Philippians

A 40-DAY BIBLE STUDY

"This daily devotional is something I've longed for. It is expositional, theological, and practical as it walks verse by verse through a book of the Bible in just 40 days. With such an outstanding stable of contributors, it is certain to become widely used in the days to come."

DANIEL L. AKIN,
president, Southeastern Baptist Theological Seminary,
North Carolina

"I cannot think of a greater gift to the church than a biblically rooted devotional series, which spans the entire New Testament. Christians need to study the Bible, and they need to read it devotionally, prayerfully, and expecting God's power to manifest through their reading of the pages of Scripture. The Planted in the Word series—which works through the Bible book by book, chapter by chapter, and line by line—will nourish the faith of Christians in a profound way for many years to come."

R. ALBERT MOHLER,
president, The Southern Baptist Theological Seminary,
Kentucky

"Let's be honest: daily Bible reading and prayer can get stale and tiresome. We need a fresh angle! The Planted in the Word volumes provide it. Seasoned scholars explain the text, relate it to Christ, apply it, and offer a sample prayer. Additional questions facilitate personal growth or group discussion. This is a treasure chest of Bible exposition, not random but rather in the flow of each biblical book. Follow these guides for a clearer grasp of Scripture, direction in living it out, and motivation for rich, Scripture-grounded communion with God."

ROBERT W. YARBROUGH,
professor of New Testament, Covenant Theological Seminary,
Missouri

"As a pastor, I'm constantly seeking resources that help our congregation dive deeper into the Scriptures—reading, understanding, and living out God's Word. The Planted in the Word series delivers this in an outstanding way. The level of scholarship throughout is truly exceptional, and I have great trust and respect for each of the contributors. I'm excited to place these valuable tools in the hands of our church members, knowing they will be well-equipped to grow in their faith."

JASON DEES,
senior pastor, Christ Covenant,
Atlanta, Georgia

Philippians

A 40-DAY BIBLE STUDY

ANDREW M. DAVIS

Benjamin L. Merkle, Series Editor

Philippians: A 40-Day Bible Study
Planted in the Word, edited by Benjamin L. Merkle

Lexham Press, 1313 Commercial St., Bellingham, WA 98225
LexhamPress.com

Print ISBN 9781683597841
Digital ISBN 9781683597858
Library of Congress Control Number 2024946840

Series Editor: Benjamin L. Merkle
Lexham Editorial: Elliot Ritzema, Allisyn Ma, Mandi Newell
Cover Design: Joshua Hunt
Typesetting: ProjectLuz.com

24 25 26 27 28 29 30 / US / 12 11 10 9 8 7 6 5 4 3 2 1

Contents

Series Preface

The longest book of the Bible begins by describing someone who is blessed (Ps 1:1–3). Such a person does not walk with the wicked, stand with sinners, or sit with scoffers. Instead, they delight in God's law, meditating on it day and night. They are further described as a tree that is located in an ideal setting—it is planted by streams of water. Water brings nourishment and sustenance to a tree. Without water, a tree will wither and die. But with sufficient water comes growth, causing the tree to produce its fruit. Where the tree is planted makes all the difference. If it is planted by a stream, it has a continual source of life-giving water.

God's word is the water that nourishes the soul. Without it, we spiritually wither or shrivel, and in order to continue "life as normal" we are forced to draw sustenance from other places—places that were never designed to give us what only God can. The goal of this series is to help you experience God's blessing by planting you beside the stream of God's life-giving word. Each volume consists of forty days of guided Bible study through a particular book (or books) of the New Testament. And each day's study consists of five components:

1. *Read* the passage of Scripture.

2. *Meditate* on the meaning of the text.

3. *Reflect on Christ*, since all the promises of God are "yes" and "amen" in him (2 Cor 1:20).
4. *Apply God's Word* because it is alive and active, and is what God uses to transform us into the image of his Son.
5. *Pray*, asking for God's help.

Additionally, the *Study It Further* section provides a way for you to dig deeper by examining how the Old Testament provides the background for the passage, by looking at a particular word or theme elsewhere in the New Testament, or by encouraging you to consider how the passage relates to you personally.

So, drink deeply from God's word. Let us not be like those who are influenced by the things of this world, causing us to drift further and further away from God (from walking, to standing, and eventually to sitting with the wicked). Instead, let us be planted in the word, drawing continual nourishment for our souls through the life-giving and fruit-producing words of the living God.

Benjamin L. Merkle
Series Editor

Introduction to Philippians

The night before Christ died, he spoke timeless words to his disciples, preparing them for what was to come. He said, "I am the vine; you are the branches. Whoever abides in me and I in him, he it is that bears much fruit, for apart from me, you can do nothing" (John 15:5). Just as a branch must stay physically connected to the vine to get the life-giving sap that flows from the root system, so all Christians must stay spiritually connected to the Savior to stay alive and bear eternal fruit for his kingdom. Jesus made it clear in John that we abide in him by having his words abide in our hearts and having our hearts lifted up consistently in prayer (John 15:7). That is where this devotional comes in. The discipline of a daily time in God's word and prayer is essential to our spiritual life and fruitfulness in Christ. Forty days in Philippians will deeply enrich your soul and prepare you for fruitfulness day after day.

The book of Philippians is brief, only 104 verses. Yet it brings the reader into powerful themes that are indispensable to our full fruitfulness in Christ. More than anything, it is an "attitude" book, pointing the way to a consistently joyful, peaceful, and trusting attitude in Christ. It commands us to have the humble mind of Christ in serving God and others. Again and again it commands joy in Christ, enabling Christians to shine like stars in a world darkened by sin (Phil 2:15). By drinking in the timeless truths locked in these 104 verses over the next forty days, you will be led to an unshakable Christian contentment that will offer hope to a hopeless generation.

PHILIPPI: THE CITY AND ITS PEOPLE

Philippi was the most significant city in Macedonia (Acts 16:12), the northernmost part of Greece. It had been named after Philip of Macedon, father of Alexander the Great, in 356 BC. It was strategically located at the eastern end of a beautiful, fertile plain, and running through the middle was the Egnatian Way—the major highway that connected Rome with the eastern portions of her empire. Because of its history with various Roman generals and significant battles, the city had been designated a colony of Rome, making all of its inhabitants Roman citizens. This heritage gave rise to a powerful loyalty to the emperor and the common confession that Caesar was "Lord" and "Savior."

This background of Roman citizenship was undoubtedly on Paul's mind when he reminded the Philippian Christians that their true Lord was Jesus (Phil 2:11), their true citizenship was in heaven, and the true salvation was resurrection in a glorious body into a perfect world (Phil 3:20–21).

THE PHILIPPIAN CHURCH: ITS FOUNDING AND ITS CHALLENGES

The founding of the Philippian church was wrapped in the supernatural power of God. The account is given for us in Acts 16:9–40. It began with God's guidance to Paul and his missionary team (including Silas, Timothy, and Luke) in the form of a vision of a man of Macedonia begging, "Come over to Macedonia and help us" (Acts 16:9). Paul followed that vision and soon found a group of women, including a wealthy woman named Lydia, who were praying at a river. Paul led Lydia and other members of her household to Christ and used her estate as a base of operations. Persecution arose, however, when Paul and Silas drove a demon out of a slave girl who used to make money for her owners by fortune-telling. Her owners were incensed at the loss of income and dragged Paul and Silas before the Roman judge. He beat them publicly without a trial and threw them in jail, not knowing that they were Roman citizens.

During the night, while Paul and Silas were in the darkened jail with bleeding backs and their feet locked up in the stocks, they began singing praises to the Lord, and all the other prisoners were listening to them. God sent an earthquake, which caused the prison doors to fly open and everyone's chains to fall off, though no one left the jail. The Philippian jailer was about to kill himself, thinking all his prisoners had escaped. Paul called out to save both this man's life and his eternal soul when the jailer asked the key question, "What must I do to be saved?" Paul and Silas preached the gospel's answer: "Believe in the Lord Jesus, and you will be saved, you and your household" (Acts 16:31). The jailer and his family received the Lord and were baptized. These events comprise the supernatural founding of the Philippian church, which scholars date around AD 49.

We also learn from this epistle that this church has been lavishly, financially generous to Paul from the time the members became Christians. And they continued to support him, having sent one of their members, Epaphroditus, with their financial gift (Phil 4:18).

But now, they were facing significant challenges. These came in two categories: challenges from outside the church and challenges from within. Of the challenges outside the church, the same hate-filled pagan persecutors who opposed Paul and Silas were still there. Paul says of them, "Their god is their belly" (Phil 3:19). Paul also wants the Philippians to beware of the threat of those who belonged to a party called the Judaizers, who were teaching a false gospel combining faith in Christ with Jewish legalism, beginning with circumcision (Phil 3:1–2). The internal challenges were the sin natures of the Philippians themselves: their selfishness, quarrelling, and disunity (Phil 2:1–3; 4:2–3). But Paul especially zeroes in on their terror of persecution and their fear of death. Combining both aspects—external and internal—Paul says he wants the Philippians to live their daily lives in a manner worthy of the gospel, standing firm in one spirit, contending for the faith of the gospel, not frightened in any way by their enemies (Phil 1:27–28). This is the central exhortation of the book.

THE APOSTLE PAUL: HIS IMPRISONMENT, HIS GRATITUDE, AND HIS PASTORAL HEART

Paul's own circumstances are dramatic and poignant. Once again, he is in chains for Christ, this time probably in Rome. He mentions the progress of the gospel throughout the whole Praetorian Guard. These were the choicest soldiers in the Roman army primarily entrusted with the task of being Caesar's bodyguards. Though these elite soldiers were found throughout the empire, the fact that Paul mentions the *whole* guard (Phil 1:13) strongly implies he was imprisoned in Rome. Scholars estimate the date of the letter to be around AD 62.

Paul writes first and foremost to express deep thanks for the Philippians' gift but also to teach them an important lesson on Christian contentment. This shows his pastoral heart throughout the epistle. He wants to do everything he can to strengthen the faith of the Philippians. He speaks courageously of his own imprisonment and how it has led to the spread of the gospel. He also speaks clearly of his own drive to know Christ better, especially in suffering, so that he can be perfectly conformed to Christ in all respects.

THE CENTRAL INSIGHT: JOY IN THE JOURNEYS

In this brief epistle, therefore, Paul sets before the Philippian Christians, and indeed the Holy Spirit sets before all Christians in every generation, two infinite journeys. Philippians 1:25 speaks of progress *in the gospel*—sanctification, or growth into being more like Christ. Philippians 1:12 speaks of the progress *of the gospel*—through evangelism. The word "progress" (*prokopē*) implies a journey. The two journeys implied here are the internal journey of growth in Christlike maturity and the external journey of growth in the spread of the gospel to lost people.

But making progress in each of these two journeys is not all Paul has in mind in this beautiful epistle. More than anything, he wants them to display *joy* in those two journeys: to rejoice in the Lord always, in any and all circumstances, whether in life or even in death. Philippians is an attitude book, instructing and exhorting all Christians to display a supernatural joy that can only be explained by the Spirit of God's work within them. Twelve times in this brief epistle he displays, mentions, or commands joy (Phil 1:4, 18, 25; 2:2, 17, 18, 28, 29; 4:1, 4, 10 [2x]). In the midst of it all, Paul has the healthiest possible mentality toward both life and death: "For to me to live is Christ, and to die is gain" (Phil 1:21). Knowing that Christ's resurrection has defeated death forever and that eternal joy is waiting for us in heaven enables us to face all dangers without fear.

Day 1

Philippians 1:1–2

READE

Paul and Timothy, servants of Christ Jesus, To all the saints in Christ Jesus who are at Philippi, with the overseers and deacons: Grace to you and peace from God our Father and the Lord Jesus Christ.

MEDITATE

Today we begin our exciting forty-day journey through the timeless and perfect epistle of Paul to the Philippians, written almost two thousand years ago but still ready to minister grace to God's people today! And it is a journey of grace, as all of Paul's epistles begin with the same phrase, "Grace to you." Grace begins as a settled determination in the mind of God before the foundation of the world to do his chosen people infinite good, though they deserve infinite wrath. Grace then flows out in numberless tributaries to the hearts, bodies, and circumstances of the elect, completing their salvation and making them maximally fruitful in this world. All of those rivers of grace come from God our Father and have been purchased by the blood of the Lord Jesus Christ. And few of those rivers of grace are as powerful as this epistle to the Philippians.

Paul adds Timothy to the author line, though the letter is clearly from Paul (he uses "I," "me," and "my" throughout). But he wants the Philippian Christians to see this gospel work as an amazing collaborative endeavor by all of God's saints. These first two verses make plain some key conceptions all Christians should have of themselves. We are all "servants of Jesus Christ," joyfully obligated to obey his every command. We are all "saints in Christ Jesus," showing our eternal position as holy and blameless through faith in Christ. And we all have some specific location to which God has called us to serve his interests. In the audience's case, they were "in Philippi." As you read this, you are almost certainly not "in Philippi," but you are positioned somewhere in God's world to serve God's purposes. This epistle is given as "grace to you" to help finish your own salvation (see 2:12–13) and make you wealthy in "the fruit that increases to your credit" (see 4:17).

My prayer for you is that this forty-day journey in Philippians will do in your life exactly what Paul wanted it to do for the original recipients of his letter: minister "grace to you and peace." If you are already a Christian, this grace will come to further your sanctification, your holiness in Christ. It has the power to make you joyful in whatever state you are in. It can also convict you to courageously share the gospel to those in your location, and it can give you peace—a feeling of peacefulness that will guard your heart and mind through Christ Jesus. If you are not yet a Christian, it has the power to minister saving grace to your soul, and grant a status of peace with God—the full forgiveness of all your sins. All these blessings can flow to you day by day as you feed on this sweet epistle by faith in Christ Jesus.

REFLECT ON CHRIST

It is vital that we realize, every moment of our lives, that every spiritual blessing we have in this world and the next comes through the Lord Jesus Christ alone. To say that this grace is purchased by the blood of Christ should make us think of the agonies that the Lord endured at Gethsemane and Calvary for us. This sense of the infinite price of our salvation humbles us and makes us ready to serve him sacrificially. We are all so prideful, and our pride rises up daily to challenge God's will for our lives. Nothing has the power to slay our pride as much as a deep meditation on the sufferings of Christ for our salvation. As you meditate, picture him sweating great drops of blood in Gethsemane. Picture him pierced for our transgressions on Calvary. Then picture him standing before you in resurrection glory, saying, "As the Father has sent me, even so I am sending you" (John 20:21). This has the power to drive away that selfishness we all have that persuades us that this day is ours to spend as we see fit without first kneeling before our Lord.

APPLY GOD'S WORD

Take a moment to meditate on grace. First, remember that God the Father has loved us with an everlasting love (Jer 31:3) in Christ. That is the foundation of the constant joy that this epistle will mention again and again.

Second, ready your soul for the feast of grace that comes by God's word. Our salvation is not yet complete. Paul will say plainly, "work out your own salvation with fear and trembling" (Phil 2:12). That always begins with God's word flowing into our hearts by the Holy Spirit. Realize that you must be in God's word every single day to keep growing in Christ.

Third, ask the Lord what he would have you do today. Tell him that you are his servant, ready to do his will. Present yourself to him, ready to obey. Ask him to remind you to do that throughout the day—mid-morning, at lunchtime, later in the afternoon, as evening falls, before you turn in at night, and many other times besides. Train yourself to live every moment for his will and watch your joy increase and your fruitfulness abound!

PRAY

Gracious Father, I yearn to please you with the meditations of my heart and the actions of my body. Pour out your grace to me in Christ! Strengthen me, and not me only, but the leaders in my church. May your grace protect them and enable them to lead and to serve for your glory alone! Amen.

STUDY IT FURTHER

1. Read 1 Corinthians 15:10. What does that verse teach about the grace of God in Paul's life? How does God's grace cause him to work hard in his Christian life and service but also to realize that apart from Christ he can do nothing? How does that concept help you understand grace better?

2. Paul frequently called himself a "slave" or "servant" of Christ (see Rom 1:1; 2 Cor 4:5; Titus 1:1). Philippians 2:7 calls Jesus a "servant" of God in his incarnation. What does this concept teach you about the Christian life? Why do we find it hard to act like a servant of God and others?

3. What can you learn from Paul's fatherly relationship with Timothy, especially including him in the heading of this great epistle even though Paul clearly wrote it? How can you develop a similar relationship with a younger person in the church?

Day 2

Philippians 1:3–5

READ

I thank my God in all my remembrance of you, always in every prayer of mine for you all making my prayer with joy, because of your partnership in the gospel from the first day until now.

MEDITATE

One of the greatest blessings of the Christian life is prayer—the fact that Christ's death has opened for us "a new and living way" (Heb 10:20) into the very throne room of almighty God. But as Scripture makes plain, we don't always know what to pray for (Rom 8:26). The Holy Spirit has assisted us by the amazing prayer ministry of the apostle Paul. Enough details of his prayer life flowed through his pen into his epistles that we have a clear idea of some things to pray for. (We will see this more in three days, when we look at verses 9–11 of this chapter.) Here, we learn the importance of constancy and thanksgiving in prayer.

Concerning constancy, Paul speaks of "all my remembrance" of the Philippians. He refers to "every prayer of mine" for them as he prays with joy. Paul bathed people in prayer. He constantly prayed for the churches he planted. He never let up for a single day. He prayed without ceasing, knowing that their spiritual danger was relentless. This is very convicting because we can be tempted to be lazy and minimalist in our prayer lives.

Paul's theology of thankfulness is also very instructive. He considers God ultimately responsible for everything he thanks God for in prayer. Here, he thanks God for the Philippians themselves—they are all the creation of God, knit together in their mothers' wombs. He also thanks God for their salvation, for without his sovereign grace in their lives, they would still be living under his wrath. Paul especially thanks God for their "fellowship in the gospel." By this he means their sacrificial financial support of his ministry from the first days of their faith until now (see 4:15–16), as proven by their new gift through Epaphroditus (4:18). Paul is mostly thankful that their sacrificial gift means their faith in Christ has survived every evil attack from the beginning until this very day. To God alone be the glory for that!

Our faith in Christ is in constant danger. Every moment of every day, the world, the flesh, and the devil conspire to destroy our faith, yet Christ is at the right hand of God interceding for us that our faith will not fail (see Luke 22:32). And the fact that it doesn't fail is proof of God's grace, which shields us and sustains us moment by moment. That is why Paul thanks God for the Philippians—because he considers their continued fellowship in the gospel as proof of God's mighty power to save his people, even though they are living every day spiritually in enemy territory. Only when we get to heaven will we find out how much God alone should be praised for our full salvation.

REFLECT ON CHRIST

Paul's demeanor of thankfulness in prayer is based on the finished work of Christ on the cross and his confidence in Christ's intercessory prayer ministry for us. Christ is the perfect mediator for us in the presence of God the Father, and he will get everything he asks from his Father because he always prays according to his Father's will. Therefore we can come to God in Christ confident and thankful in everything we pray for based on his word. This constant thankfulness in prayer should greatly sweeten our lives day by day. A truly thankful person is a joyful person, buoyant in trials, sweet in friendship, delightful in fellowship, fruitful in evangelism. All of this flows from the ministry of Christ on our behalf.

How can we ever thank God enough for what he has given us in Christ? And how can we thank Christ enough for what he was willing to suffer for us? The more we reflect on the person and work of Christ, the more thankful we will be, and that certainly extends to every Christian we know, because by Christ's work alone is each one of them saved.

APPLY GOD'S WORD

Do you labor constantly in prayer for others? Or would you say that a pattern of laziness has emerged that cuts off your prayers for Christians in your life? If so, ask God to increase your desire and frequency for prayer for the people God has brought into your world.

Are you a thankful person? Do you express that thankfulness to God regularly in prayer? I find it very convicting to realize how easily I complain to God when something goes wrong and forget to thank him for the limitless blessings I have in Christ. This theology of thankfulness is especially powerful when we apply it to other people. If you need help in this area, you may want to begin by making a list of Christians in your life for whom you are thankful. Then extend it to include Christians whose personalities and problems you find personally challenging. Thank God for them! Thank God for their faith, for their perseverance in the gospel, for the fruit God has worked and will work in their lives. The more consistently you thank God for people you're having problems with, the sweeter your disposition will be toward them and the readier you will be to serve them in love.

PRAY

O Lord, you are responsible for every good and perfect gift in our lives. Thank you for my salvation. Thank you for sustaining my faith despite the constant attacks from the world, the flesh, and the devil. Please teach me to pray more constantly and more thankfully for the ones you have brought into my life. Amen.

STUDY IT FURTHER

1. Read Romans 6:17. What does Paul thank God for there? What does that teach you about the sovereignty of God in salvation?

2. Read Luke 22:32. What does Jesus pray for concerning Simon Peter? What does this teach you about saving faith? What does it teach you about Jesus's intercessory life for us all? How does it combine with Hebrews 7:25 to teach us about Jesus's constant prayers for us?

3. What was the nature of the Philippians' partnership in the gospel? How does money factor into that? How could that challenge us to support God's work financially?

Day 3

Philippians 1:6

READ

And I am sure of this, that he who began a good work in you will bring it to completion at the day of Jesus Christ.

MEDITATE

God planned his work of salvation in our souls before time began, from eternity past—before the first man was formed from the dust, before God created the heavens and the earth, before he said, "Let there be light." But when Paul speaks of the good work that God began in our souls, he is referring to actual power poured into us, transforming us, preparing us for heaven. Before we even heard the gospel, God did a work of preparation in us, putting key elements in place that would be essential to our salvation. Then, at the right time and in the perfect way, God orchestrated events so we could hear the gospel message of Christ crucified and resurrected in an effective way. At the moment that our eardrums vibrated with the sounds of the gospel, God sent forth his Spirit into our heart, taking out the heart of stone and giving us a heart of flesh to respond in faith to the gospel (Ezek 36:26). This mighty work of new birth began our existence as a new creation (2 Cor 5:17). This is what Paul meant when he spoke to the Philippians these words, "He who began a good work *in you* ..."

In every one of his children, from the moment of conversion until he takes them out of this world, God is constantly at work, completing the salvation he began. Salvation is a process that comes to us in stages, as Paul will make plain in 2:12–13 when he commands that we work out our salvation with fear and trembling. There he will say that we do this work in mysterious partnership with the same God who is at work in us, both to will and to do for his good pleasure.

God is constantly at work in our souls, preparing us for the glory that will be ours in the next world. This work is deep and mysterious, involving our thoughts, affections, emotions, and choices. But God never forgets his business, nor loses sight of his final goal for every one of his children. He never quits on any one of his elect, no matter what sins they may commit or weaknesses they may display. Our final salvation is guaranteed by the sovereign power and relentless purpose of God. This knowledge should not make us lazy or complacent but give us the confidence that every effort we make toward growth in Christ will end in final success.

Perhaps no verse in the Bible is quoted as frequently as Philippians 1:6 to support the doctrine commonly called "once saved, always saved." Though I agree with the overall point of that doctrine, I dislike the phrase because it forgets the dynamism implied in this verse—that God has more saving work to do in us to ready us for eternal glory in Christ. Those who speak this slogan may look on all of salvation as accomplished when we're born again—as though to say, "Once justified, always justified." And while that's true, it is vital for us to realize that not one of us is done with our salvation journey; we have a road to travel. God started this transformation in us and will not stop working in a single one of his children until they are all safely in heavenly glory.

REFLECT ON CHRIST

Paul says God will carry on this mighty work of salvation in us "until the day of Jesus Christ." What does that mean? It could emphasize judgment, referring to when Christ returns in glory to end human history and destroy all his enemies. The Old Testament prophets called that "the Day of the Lord." But given that the context here is the completion of individual salvation, I think it refers to the day of Jesus Christ as the wedding of the Bride and the Bridegroom, the heavenly consummation. In Ephesians 5:25–27, we are told that "Christ loved the church and gave himself up for her, that he might sanctify her, having cleansed her by the washing of water with the word, so that he might present the church to himself in splendor, without spot or wrinkle or any such thing, that she might be holy and without blemish." That process is what Philippians 1:6 is describing, getting the Bride beautifully dressed for the Husband.

The work of holiness God is doing in our souls is readying us for that glorious wedding day when we will be eternally united with the lover of our souls, Jesus Christ.

APPLY GOD'S WORD

There is no command in Philippians 1:6. That will come later, as I have mentioned, in 2:12–13. We must work out our salvation, and that work is hard, but the application here is one of confidence. Paul says, "I am sure of this," which refers to God's commitment to finish what he started. The Greek word translated "sure" is related to persuasion. Paul has been completely persuaded of God's determination to finish our salvation. This persuasion comes from biblical meditation and from spiritual experience. Our goal then is to attain that level of confidence through our own time with the Lord. Whenever we sin, Satan will use our sins against us to discourage us. He is the "accuser of our brothers" (Rev 12:10), and he wants to crush our spirits so we stop fighting sin and serving God. At those times, use Philippians 1:6 to fight Satan.

Beyond our personal assurance, we can minister the same truth to other Christians who are downcast. God wants us to "strengthen the hands which hang down, and the feeble knees" (Heb 12:12 NKJV) of our brothers and sisters. Tell them that God is mighty to save them, and that Christ will never "grow faint or be discouraged" (Isa 42:4) until he has finished their salvation.

PRAY

God of our salvation, it is difficult for us to comprehend the magnitude of your power toward us, guaranteeing our salvation in the day of Jesus Christ. Expand our minds to understand that power more. Help us to feel the confidence that Paul expressed that you will never stop working in us until our salvation is finished. Amen.

STUDY IT FURTHER

1. Read Romans 8:29–30. How do those verses support the doctrine of the eternal security of our salvation?

2. In John 10:27–30, Jesus says that no one can snatch his sheep from his hand, or from the Father's hand. How does that passage strengthen your confidence in your own final salvation in Christ?

3. How does the doctrine of the eternal security of the believer actually help us to work hard on our own salvation (see Phil 2:12–13)?

Day 4

Philippians 1:7–8

READ

It is right for me to feel this way about you all, because I hold you in my heart, for you are all partakers with me of grace, both in my imprisonment and in the defense and confirmation of the gospel. For God is my witness, how I yearn for you all with the affection of Christ Jesus.

MEDITATE

These verses give us a glimpse into the powerful affection Paul had for his fellow brothers and sisters in Christ, as well as the unity the global body of Christ has in all gospel ministry around the world. Paul's deep love for the Philippians is evident in his language here. He says, "I hold you in my heart." He also calls God as his witness to demonstrate that he yearns for them all "with the affection of Christ Jesus." Love for the brothers and sisters in Christ is among the clearest evidences of our new nature in Christ. The apostle John made this plain in his first epistle: "We know that we have passed out of death into life, because we love the brothers" (1 John 3:14). It is even more amazing in Paul's case because on the morning of his conversion on the road to Damascus he was "breathing threats and murder" (Acts 9:1) against all Christians. He went from hating Christians to being perhaps the greatest lover of Christians in church history. Later in this same chapter, Philippians 1, Paul will say that, if given the choice between going to perfect bliss in heaven or staying and suffering on earth, he would rather stay because it would be better for his brothers and sisters if he continued with them (1:24–25). Based on that one statement, it is clear that there is nothing Paul wouldn't do for the children of God, no pain he wouldn't be willing to suffer.

Beyond that, in these two verses, we can see how Paul asserts that the Philippians were sharing with him in all the trials and successes of his ministry. Not only were they sharing in his work by supporting him financially, they were also praying for him and yearning for his release from prison and for his eternal fruitfulness in the gospel. They knew that Paul was called in a special way for "the defense and confirmation of the gospel." Paul was in chains for Christ and would be called on again and again to defend Christ before hostile tribunals. Paul called them "partakers with me of grace." They were joining in his struggles by praying for him. They loved him dearly. Even more importantly, they loved Christ dearly, and they deeply desired that the gospel spread as widely and rapidly as possible, even though that meant the suffering of Christ's choicest servants.

These beautiful verses show us the mystical unity all Christians have with one another, as well as the bond of yearning we all have that Christ be exalted in his people all over the world.

REFLECT ON CHRIST

Paul says he longs for all of the Philippian Christians "with the affection of Jesus Christ." The deep love Christians have for one another flows from our spiritual union with Christ. Our salvation conforms us to Christ in all respects. Central to this union is that we love what Christ loves and hate what Christ hates. And Christ's love for his people burns with a heat like the sun. As we are drawn more and more into Christ, we will love each other as Christ loved us. This is the very thing Christ commanded of all his followers: "A new commandment I give to you, that you love one another; just as I have loved you, you also are to love one another" (John 13:34). John made it plain that the measure of love is sacrifice: "By this we know love, that he laid down his life for us, and we ought to lay down our lives for the brothers" (1 John 3:16).

Therefore, the more we grow in Christ, the greater will be our love for other Christians and our willingness to make sacrifices for them. Because we are all naturally selfish, this is a massive change in every aspect of our lives, and it is only by the work of the Spirit in us that we can love other Christians "with the affection of Christ Jesus."

APPLY GOD'S WORD

This kind of intense, committed, sacrificial love for other Christians is a work of supernatural grace. It is something that Christ must work in us by his Spirit. Ask him today to do it in you. Confess any bitterness or brokenness you may have in a relationship with another Christian. Perhaps you know of some broken relationships in your church. Ask God to make you a peacemaker. Beyond this, ask Christ to give you opportunities to serve other Christians through self-sacrifice. Learn how to lay down your life for others.

Paul speaks here about those that are in chains "in the defense and confirmation of the gospel." There are many Christians suffering around the world in countries where Christianity is illegal. Learn more about the persecuted church.

There are many ministries that are specifically set up to make American Christians more aware of what is happening with our brothers and sisters in China, North Korea, the Horn of Africa, India, and many Muslim countries. Commit yourself to praying for these people groups as if you were their fellow prisoner (Heb 13:3).

PRAY

God our Father, we are heading to a heaven that will be a world of love. There we will love our brothers and sisters from every tribe, language, people, and nation with a perfect and powerful love. Give us more and more of that love now. Work in us the kind of deep affection that Paul describes here. Amen.

STUDY IT FURTHER

1. Go through 1 John 3 and write down all the things that chapter teaches you about love for other Christians. Why does John speak so passionately about that topic?

2. Saul of Tarsus, the persecutor, deeply hated Christians and viciously attacked them. How do you understand the radical change that happened in Paul by his conversion, specifically when it came to loving Christians? How could that transformation help you to grow in love for other Christians?

3. Read John 13:1–15. How does Jesus's example of foot washing in that passage teach you about loving other Christians? Why do you think Peter was so offended that Jesus was about to wash his feet? What does that teach you about our pride? How can God's grace help us both to serve others and to allow them to serve us?

Day 5

Philippians 1:9–11

READ

And it is my prayer that your love may abound more and more, with knowledge and all discernment, so that you may approve what is excellent, and so be pure and blameless for the day of Christ, filled with the fruit of righteousness that comes through Jesus Christ, to the glory and praise of God.

MEDITATE

Day after day, we kneel in prayer to Almighty God. Yet we feel acutely the struggle in our souls that we don't know what to pray for (Rom 8:26). The Holy Spirit was given to us to help us in our weakness in prayer, and so he does. But some of the Spirit's greatest help to our prayer lives was established centuries before we were even born in Paul's examples of his prayers in his epistles. Philippians 1:9–11 is an excellent example of prayer from Paul. We will meditate carefully on each aspect, and then put this kind of praying into practice.

First, Paul prays for the love of the Philippians, that it may abound more and more. Jonathan Edwards, in his great classic *Treatise on Religious Affections,* said that the human heart has two great capacities: first, the ability to understand things as they are, to analyze their nature; second, the capacity to be attracted to or repulsed from those things to a greater or lesser degree (liking or loving, disliking or hating). Love is an attribute of the heart and is prone to the push-pull nature of a magnet that Edwards described. Paul is praying for the Philippians to love what Christ loves more and more passionately, to be pulled in the direction of loving God, other Christians, righteousness, the work of God, and all things Christ loves.

Second, Paul prays for that love to grow in knowledge and discernment. He wants the Philippians to be rooted and grounded in sound theology and to have wise and discerning hearts. This kind of wisdom is celebrated in the Old Testament as a mark of true godliness, lived out in practical ways day to day, but it is consummated in the New Testament wisdom of Christ and his kingdom by approving "what is excellent," living in light of these spiritual realities every moment.

Third, this means being pure and blameless, putting all sin to death so that they do not offend the Holy Spirit. All sin offends the holy eyes of Almighty God, and the Holy Spirit burns within us to refine us until the day of Christ.

Fourth, Paul prays for the Philippians to be "filled with the fruit of righteousness." Fruit comes in two main categories: attitude fruit and action fruit. Attitude fruit is listed in Galatians 5:22–23 as the fruit of the Spirit, including such heart states as love, joy, peace, and patience. Action fruit involves serving others, proclaiming the gospel, alleviating suffering in this sin-cursed world. Paul wants them *filled* with such fruits, bearing an abundant harvest of righteousness.

REFLECT ON CHRIST

Such a beautiful array of spiritual blessings come only by Jesus Christ and result in the fullest display of the glory of God in our lives. Paul ends his prayer with this glory and praise of God. Every prayer ever uttered by a child of God in this world comes into God's heart only by the priestly ministry of Jesus Christ. Because he shed his blood for us, God hears our prayers. Every prayer pleasing to God ends in the purposes of God for his people, namely that they be perfectly conformed to the image of his Son, Jesus Christ (Rom 8:29). Every word of this timeless prayer that Paul uttered for the Philippians should remind every generation of Christians in the succeeding centuries to reflect on Christ and worship his glory.

APPLY GOD'S WORD

As we walk through the details of Paul's magnificent prayer for the Philippians and see how Christ-centered it is and how much it glorifies God, we can employ its lessons in our own prayer lives. Instructed by the Holy Spirit, we can no longer say, "I don't know what to pray for!" Take each element of Philippians 1:9–11 and pray it for each member of your family and for the members of your church. Extend your prayer lists further than ever before; choose Christians in strategic ministries that you are aware of and pray these specific things for them. As we already saw in Philippians 1:3, we should practice this kind of praying continually, day after day. Do not pray these things just once and then check it off the list. Kneel daily before the Father and let these words pour out of your heart, not in a mechanical, rote manner. Study the concepts behind the words and rephrase and expand them as the Spirit leads. In this way, your prayers for all the saints will be powerful and effective.

PRAY

Loving and kind Father, thank you for sending forth your Holy Spirit to teach us to pray. Apart from his perfect ministry, we would never know what to pray for, but now we do. Now make us prayer warriors in our generation as Paul was in his! Amen.

STUDY IT FURTHER

1. As you seek to improve your prayer life, go through some of the prayers of Paul in other epistles. Two great examples are in Ephesians 1:15–19 and Ephesians 3:14–21. What ideas do those prayers give you that you can implement in your own prayer life?

2. Read Jesus's amazing prayer in John 17. Zero in on Jesus's prayer for his disciples to be one as God the Father and Jesus are one. How could that prayer shape your prayer life? How could you pray for that level of unity in your family, your church, and in the Christian church around the world?

3. Read again the list of the fruit of the Spirit in Galatians 5:22–23. How could this list serve as a great basis for your prayers for others?

Day 6

Philippians 1:12

READ

I want you to know, brothers, that what has happened to me has really served to advance the gospel …

MEDITATE

Before we consider verse 13, let us first skip ahead to verse 20, where Paul states his deepest desire for his life in this world: "It is my eager expectation and hope that I will not be at all ashamed, but that with full courage now as always Christ will be honored [lit. "magnified"] in my body, whether by life or by death." Paul wants Christ to be glorified through him, even if his own death would be the best means to that end. This is truly staggering, and Paul will expound on it more in this chapter. Paul had reached the point where he considered his life worth nothing to him if he could only complete the gospel ministry Christ had given to him (Acts 20:24).

However, while he lived in the body, the best way he could magnify Christ was by making progress in two infinitely significant journeys. Both verse 12 and verse 25 ("Convinced of this, I know that I will remain and continue with you all, for your progress and joy in the faith") use the same Greek word *prokopē* ("progress" or "advancement"). The idea of making progress along a route, a way, a road, implies a journey. The first journey, in verse 12, is the journey of gospel advancement through the proclamation of the death and resurrection of Christ. This is what I call the "external journey" of evangelism and missions. The second journey, in verse 25, is the progress Paul would help the Philippians make in their Christian joy and faith. This is the "internal journey" of sanctification and growth in Christlikeness.

I call these two journeys "infinite" because they will continue to stretch out before us while we live in this world, only the infinite power of God can accomplish them, and they result in an eternity of glory in the presence of God. Growth into greater and greater Christlikeness will never end in this world, for it involves a total transformation of our minds and hearts resulting in a constant change in our actions. Until God completes that transformation through our glorification, we have progress to make. So also, the gospel work of evangelism and missions will stretch out before the worldwide church until the second coming of Christ. There will always be lost people around us and lost people groups in distant lands who have never heard the name of Christ.

Paul's priority structure should define our lives in our earthly bodies as well. We should live so that Christ is magnified in us no matter what the cost. To accomplish this, we should give ourselves daily to leading lost people to Christ (progress *of* the gospel) and to growing ourselves and helping other Christians to grow in Christlikeness (progress *in* the gospel).

REFLECT ON CHRIST

I love the concept of "magnifying Christ" through my body. To magnify Christ does not mean to make him any greater, for he is infinitely great. As the telescope does not make Saturn's rings any larger but only makes them more visible, so our lives in this world should serve to make Christ's infinite greatness more visible to those who see us. The reason Saturn's massive rings are invisible to the naked eye is because of the immense distance. In the same way, Christ appears so small to sinners—who see him as a good moral teacher, or a guru, or a wise man, or even a Savior (without any true realization of what that means)—but as we live openly for Christ and boldly evangelize, some of God's lost sheep will see more and more of his infinite glory and will yearn to know him.

As we gaze on the majestic greatness of Christ in the word, it should create within each Christian a yearning to be like him. It will draw us closer to him, and we will realize how much we have underestimated his glory ourselves. As the Spirit works in us, he will use this spiritual gaze to transform us from glory into glory (2 Cor 3:18). This is progress in the internal journey. As we are conformed to Christ's heart for the lost, it will make us willing to lay down our lives for his sheep as evangelists, willing to suffer whatever is needed to see them saved.

APPLY GOD'S WORD

Each of us must be committed to making daily progress in these two journeys: the internal journey of sanctification and the external journey of gospel advancement through evangelism and missions. These two journeys have the same goal in the end—the fulfillment of the Great Commission Christ gave to make disciples, baptize them, and teach them to obey everything he has commanded (Matt 28:19–20). It was for this purpose that Christ left his people in this world.

First and foremost, ask the Lord to work in you the same level of commitment that Paul had that Christ be magnified in your body, whether by life or death. Second, ask him to grow you in grace and in the knowledge of Christ (2 Pet 3:18), making you more and more Christlike with each passing day. Third, ask him to give you opportunities to step out boldly and share the gospel with someone who is lost in their sins. Though this will be costly, the Spirit will give you power to be fruitful.

PRAY

Our Father, enable us now to live moment by moment that the glory of your Son might be magnified in our bodies. Help us to make progress in the two journeys: help us grow in Christlikeness and give us boldness to lead others to Christ. Amen.

STUDY IT FURTHER

1. Psalm 34:3 says, "Oh, magnify the LORD with me, and let us exalt his name together!" What does it mean for us to magnify the Lord? How do we display his greatness? How do we do this with other Christians? How would thinking about this affect our worship lives?

2. Read the Great Commission in Matthew 28:18–20. How is the fulfillment of this an "infinite journey"? Explore the history of missions and seek to find how the spread of the gospel from Jerusalem to the distant parts of the earth has been a journey for the church. How is the Lord leading you to get involved in it?

3. What is the difference between external progress *of* the gospel and internal progress *in* the gospel? How can we be involved in doing both? How does our progress in each of these ways greatly glorify God?

Day 7

Philippians 1:13–14

READ

… so that it has become known throughout the whole imperial guard and to all the rest that my imprisonment is for Christ. And most of the brothers, having become confident in the Lord by my imprisonment, are much more bold to speak the word without fear.

MEDITATE

In our last study, I introduced the central priorities of Paul's life: the glory of Christ in the progress of the two journeys, namely, the external journey of gospel advancement and the internal journey of sanctification—progress *of* the gospel and progress *in* the gospel. Today, we zero in on the specific circumstances of Paul's imprisonment and how Paul saw it. So much of the book of Philippians displays godly attitudes in any and every circumstance, including persecution for the gospel. Paul wants the Philippians to know that God has surprisingly used his imprisonment for the furtherance of the gospel. This has happened in two senses: first, Paul used his imprisonment for Christ as a platform to preach the gospel to those in prison, both to the palace guard and to the other prisoners; second, Paul's example of faith-filled suffering gave boldness to other Christians to share the gospel as well.

Paul's faith-filled and fruitful ministry in chains would by no means have been a new concept to the Philippian church. Acts 16 records the circumstances of Paul and Silas's unjust public beating and imprisonment for the gospel, their cheerful worship in the middle of the night, the miraculous earthquake that killed no one, and the subsequent salvation of the Philippian jailer and his family. Given all this, the fact that Paul's faithfulness for Christ has led to yet another imprisonment would not have surprised them, nor would his faith-filled response to that suffering. Paul's captive audience of his fellow prisoners and even the palace guard would all hear the gospel from his lips.

The palace guard is the praetorium, the personal bodyguards of the emperor. These were some of the bravest and most trusted soldiers in the entire Roman army. At the end of the epistle, Paul will speak of some converts who were "of Caesar's household" (4:22). I am confident that Paul's ministry to the palace guards would have been instrumental in such conversions.

Paul speaks of the boldness of other Christian brothers because of his chains. This is a clear display of the power of Christian leadership. Picture a military commander who leads from the front, courageously braving enemy fire while he waves his sword and yells, "Come on, men, let's go!" Paul braved among the greatest levels of sufferings ever recorded in church history, some of which are listed in 2 Corinthians 11:23–28. He was savagely beaten or whipped at least eight times; at least three times, enemies of the gospel started riots because of his preaching; and we know that some Jews bound themselves by an oath that they would not eat until they had assassinated Paul

(Acts 23:12). When the onlooking Christians saw this level of commitment and boldness in the gospel, many of them lost their fear and preached Christ boldly as well.

The Holy Spirit intended for every generation since Paul's time to have the same boldness in evangelism and missions. Therefore, he inspired Luke to write the accounts in Acts and Paul to record his words in his epistles. The Spirit knows our weaknesses and is ready to give us power to be Christ's witnesses in our day (Acts 1:8).

REFLECT ON CHRIST

Paul says plainly that his chains are "for Christ" (1:13). It is because of Paul's faith in Christ that he was arrested. Christ bids his followers to come and die, to take up our cross daily and follow him (Luke 9:23). No call in the Christian life is harder or more fruitful. Jesus himself said, "Unless a grain of wheat falls into the earth and dies, it remains alone; but if it dies, it bears much fruit" (John 12:24). Every fiber of our natural being tends toward self-preservation. We love our lives in this world. But Jesus calls us to hate our lives in this world, so that we may gain eternal glory (John 12:25). The resurrected Christ appeared to Paul on the Damascus road and put a lasting vision of his glory in Paul's mind. From then on, Paul yearned to know Christ and make him known. This is the best remedy to the fear we all have in evangelism—a desire for Christ to be glorified in the lives of lost people. Love for Christ and his sheep drives out fear.

APPLY GOD'S WORD

It is time for all of us to face our fears in evangelism and overcome them by the power of the Holy Spirit. Paul's boldness and chains are a permanent source of inspiration to every generation of Christians. When those who knew Paul personally saw how he carried himself in chains, many of them lost all fear and spoke the gospel boldly. Those who responded by faith to their words are now with them in heaven, falling before Christ's heavenly throne and drinking in Christ's heavenly glory. It is the very thing Jesus prayed for in John 17:24: "Father, I desire that they also, whom you have given me, may be with me where I am, to see my glory." For that to happen, Christ's servants on earth must be willing to die to ourselves and to our desire for an easy life. We must be willing to speak boldly to those who are perishing and proclaim the simple gospel of Christ crucified and risen.

Ask the Lord to send his Spirit upon you today and give you an opportunity to speak the words of life to someone. It may be a coworker, a neighbor, a relative, an acquaintance on your (or your child's) sports team, a roommate, someone sitting next to you on a plane, or a total stranger. Ask the Lord to give you the same boldness he gave to Paul's friends in his day.

PRAY

Lord of the harvest, send out your laborers into the harvest field. Allow me to be one of them. People around me are lost and in need. Please give me the boldness I need to speak the gospel to them today. Amen.

STUDY IT FURTHER

1. How does the account of Paul and Silas in the Philippian jail (Acts 16) put their supernatural boldness and courage front and center? How could their example inspire you to make courageous steps for the gospel?

2. Read Acts 22. How does that chapter display Paul's amazing courage and boldness in the gospel? How does it also display the savage opposition that Paul endured for the gospel?

3. Look up the life of Adoniram Judson, the nineteenth-century missionary to Burma. What happened to him as he sought to win many Burmese people to Christ?

Day 8

Philippians 1:15–20

READ

Some indeed preach Christ from envy and rivalry, but others from good will. The latter do it out of love, knowing that I am put here for the defense of the gospel. The former proclaim Christ out of selfish ambition, not sincerely but thinking to afflict me in my imprisonment. What then? Only that in every way, whether in pretense or in truth, Christ is proclaimed, and in that I rejoice. Yes, and I will rejoice, for I know that through your prayers and the help of the Spirit of Jesus Christ this will turn out for my deliverance, as it is my eager expectation and hope that I will not be at all ashamed, but that with full courage now as always Christ will be honored in my body, whether by life or by death.

MEDITATE

In verses 15–18, Paul describes a remarkable situation connected with his imprisonment for the gospel. It seems that some people were preaching the true gospel from malicious motives, trying to add to Paul's affliction, perhaps seeking to stir up more trouble for him as a threat to the Roman Empire.

This is very different than the circumstances Paul addressed in Galatians in which some men were preaching a false gospel combining Christ's death with human obedience to the law for salvation. In that case, Paul called down eternal damnation on them, saying, "If anyone is preaching to you a gospel contrary to the one you received, let him be accursed" (Gal 1:9). A false gospel saves no souls and has the power to shipwreck those who began by believing the true gospel. In Philippians 1, these malicious people were preaching the true gospel, for Paul actually rejoices that "Christ is preached" (Phil 1:18).

We may ask, "How can malicious people preach the true gospel?" But even demons can testify to Christ and the gospel. Repeatedly Jesus had to stop demons from proclaiming who he was, as in Mark 1:24, when a demon cried out, "I know who you are—the Holy One of God." Also a demon-possessed girl followed Paul and Silas in Philippi, crying aloud, "These men are servants of the Most High God, who proclaim to you the way of salvation" (Acts 16:17). Scripture shows us that some of Satan's human servants can accurately preach Christ crucified and resurrected, from false motives.

Look at Paul's dismissive attitude of these preachers with wrong motivations. He says, "What then?" Or as we would say, "So what?" Paul cared very little for his own safety but cared enormously for the spread of the true gospel, even if it was done from false motives. As always, throughout this epistle, Paul speaks of his joy: "... in that I rejoice. Yes, and I will rejoice" (v. 18).

Of course, not everyone preaching Christ at that time was doing it from false motives. As we saw yesterday, Paul delights that some genuine servants of Christ were emboldened by his suffering to preach clearly and with great courage. The false witnesses thought they were so clever, outwitting the great apostle

Paul. Meanwhile, Paul was smiling in his cell as he heard their message, gladdened that God had possibly saved some poor sinners through their scheme!

Now it will matter greatly on Judgment Day not only what people did but why they did it. God can bless the true proclamation of his word greatly, while recording the hypocrisy and disobedience of many who preached it. God spoke his word through Balaam's donkey. God also spoke a true prophecy about Christ through the mouth of Caiaphas, the wicked high priest of Christ's day (John 11:49–52). In the same way, many corrupt church leaders through the ages have preached the word for money or power or lust. Others have violated God's biblical principles for who should preach, yet God used them anyway. God will sort it all out on the day of Christ.

REFLECT ON CHRIST

It is so powerful to see Paul's joy that "Christ is proclaimed." This simple phrase sums up the gospel in Paul's mind. Jesus Christ *is* the gospel! To preach the glories of Christ in his incarnation, and his sinless life, and his amazing miracles, and his powerful teachings, and his sacrificial death on the cross, and his mighty resurrection from the dead—to preach Christ is to preach the gospel, and that Christ-centered message is the "power of God for salvation to everyone who believes" (Rom 1:16). I can picture Paul's face wet with tears as he heard Christ being preached—the delights of his Savior, the infinite depths of his person, and the radiant glory of his being.

Every child of God should yearn for the same thing from their preachers. Every sermon should in some sense distill into this central message: "Christ is proclaimed." I know that preachers want to be faithful to the text and explain it with exegetical soundness, even if it never mentions anything about

Jesus. But in the end, the text should bring the faithful person of God in the pulpit to the glorious topic of Christ crucified and resurrected. Such preaching saves souls, both in justification and sanctification.

APPLY GOD'S WORD

How does Paul apply this for himself? He says it gives him confidence that Christ being preached so clearly "will turn out for his deliverance," especially as the Philippians would be faithful to pray for him and God would be faithful to pour out the Spirit of Jesus Christ on him. What is this deliverance? To be rescued from fear and be faithful to Christ to the end of his days (vv. 19–20).

We should yearn for Christ to be preached to our souls so that we can lose all fear of man and fear of death and be faithful to preach Christ in whatever setting God has called us to. We have already discussed this zeal for evangelism and missions several times in this devotional, but here the application is that hearing Christ preached, and receiving prayer and the help of the Spirit, is the remedy for fear in our generation, just as it was in Paul's.

So, fill your heart with Christ crucified. Seek prayers from others that you will not be ashamed of Christ. Look to the Spirit's power to give you courage. And then, proclaim Christ to the people in your life.

PRAY

My Lord, you poured out the Spirit on Paul, delivering him from fear and empowering him to speak boldly for Christ in his day. We need the same outpouring in our day! Deliver us, as you delivered Paul, from caring more what people think about us than about your glory and the salvation of people. Amen.

STUDY IT FURTHER

1. Read 2 Timothy 4:16–18. There Paul talks about his trial before Caesar and that all his friends abandoned him. But he says that the Lord stood at his side and gave him strength so that the gospel message might be fully proclaimed. He says, "I was rescued from the lion's mouth." In that Paul fully expected to be killed very soon, this rescue must mean something other than deliverance from the death penalty. Rather, the "lion" was Satan who sought to use his fears of death to keep Paul from preaching the gospel to Caesar. How does that teach you about Paul's "deliverance" here in Philippians 1? How can we grow in our boldness and courage in preaching the gospel?

2. Read John 12:24. How does that passage give you a sense of the dying that is necessary for the spread of the gospel? How does God reward people willing to die like that (John 12:26)?

3. Paul mentions the prayers of the Philippians for him. How did God use the prayers of the church to deliver Peter from prison and death in Acts 12:1–17? How could we grow in praying for persecuted Christians and their imprisoned pastors?

Day 9

Philippians 1:21

READ

For to me to live is Christ, and to die is gain.

REFLECT ON CHRIST

This is one of the most powerful statements ever uttered by the apostle Paul. I believe it is also the healthiest possible way any human being can look at life alongside death. Many Christians struggle to hold life and death in a healthy balance. Sometimes they can become weary of life in this world and yearn to live no longer—not that they are suicidal, just that all delight in life has gone entirely from them. Perhaps a loved one died, and their grief has consumed all joy in this world. Perhaps they have a chronic illness that makes even simple physical movement agony. Perhaps they have failed again and again in life's endeavors. Perhaps they are overwhelmingly lonely and feel that no one could ever love them. Life can seem so tedious in comparison to death.

On the other hand, Christians can have an unhealthy view of death. They seek to preserve their lives in this world and think very little of heaven. Once, a rich man gave John Wesley a tour of his lush estate and asked him, "Well, what do you think?" Wesley answered, "I think you will have a hard time leaving it." Death for such a person is a dreaded interruption to their happiness. Many Christians, even if they are not so wealthy, are still concerned too much with earthly health and comfort. Therefore, they avoid any mention of death.

Paul's triumphant declaration in Philippians 1:21 is the perfect remedy to both sides of this equation. He loved life in the healthiest way, and he also loved death in the healthiest way.

First, Paul's view on life: "For me to live is Christ ..." What Paul meant by this is that every day of life was an opportunity to learn more about Christ, as he will say with majestic, soaring language in Philippians 3:8–10. All he wanted was to "gain Christ" and to "know him and the power of his resurrection, and [to] share his sufferings." Along with this, every day was a chance to serve Christ and his people, his "fruitful labor" (1:22). To learn how to love and live and die to self and rise again in glory—and most of all to know Christ in all these things—that is what "to live is Christ" means.

Now, Paul's view on death: "... to die is gain." This statement would be blasphemous statement if not understood properly. The word "gain" implies increase, improvement, enrichment, profit. But Paul just said, "For me to live is Christ ..."! At face value, it seems like he is saying to die is something *better than Christ*, an improvement to Christ, greater wealth than Christ. But that is not at all what Paul means. There could be nothing better in this life or the next than Christ! Paul means, "For me to live is Christ and to die is *more Christ*!" That is the centerpiece of true Christian theology on heaven. Heaven is an ocean of the glory of God in Christ. Revelation 21:23 speaks of the infinite glories of the new Jerusalem: "The city has no need of sun or moon to shine on it, for the glory of God gives it light, and its lamp is the Lamb." Paul expects that when he dies he will have an infinitely greater experience of Christ than he ever had in this world. In 1 Corinthians 13:12, he says, "For now we see in a mirror dimly, but then face to face. Now I know in part; then I shall know fully, even as I have been fully known."

Heaven will be an infinite leap in blessedness for all the children of God, and Christ is the center of that blessedness. Heaven will be an eternal education in the glory of God as illuminated by Christ. We will never be omniscient; therefore, we will always be capable of learning Christ's glories more and more, and that is eternal "gain." You cannot have a healthier view of life or death than this.

The great missionary to Burma (Myanmar) Adoniram Judson suffered immensely for the gospel, but he also saw immense fruit in the lives of countless converts. As he lay dying, he said, "I am not tired of my work, neither am I tired of the world; yet, when Christ calls me home, I shall go with the gladness of a boy bounding away from his school." That was his version of "for me to live is Christ, and to die is gain."[1]

APPLY GOD'S WORD

Meditate deeply on this one simple statement, "For me to live is Christ, and to die is gain." Ask the Lord to reveal to you how you view both life and death in light of this verse. Ask him to make you as healthy as Paul was in his perspective on both life and death. Ask God to make knowing Christ and serving him every single day of your life the center of your existence until you draw your final breath. And ask him to give you a healthy view of heaven—your eternal education in the glories of Christ; your eternal immersion in the infinite ocean of his being; your

1. Pat Williams and Jim Denney, *What Are You Living For?* (Ventura, CA: Regal, 2008), 36.

eternal feast at the table of his mercies; your eternal worship at the limitless displays of his power.

PRAY

My gracious God, I yearn for Paul's statement, "For me to live is Christ, and to die is gain," to be deeply imprinted on my soul every day. I want to see both life and death in balance in my life. Work this in me for my maximum joy and fruitfulness for the rest of my brief time on earth. Amen.

STUDY IT FURTHER

1. Read Revelation 21. How does that magnificent chapter give you a sense of the glories of heaven awaiting all Christians in eternity? How would meditating on the infinite glories of Christ on display in heaven help you lose your fear of death? How do you expect to spend eternity in heaven? How would believing that "Christ is gain" help you live more boldly and freely in this world?

2. Missionary and martyr Jim Elliot once said, "He is no fool who gives up what he cannot keep to gain what he cannot lose." What did he mean? How does Philippians 1:21 line up with that statement? Research Jim Elliot's life and death. What did he give up for the gospel? What did he gain?

3. Why do you think some people lose interest in life? How could Philippians 1:21 help them have new life in Christ?

Day 10

Philippians 1:22–26

READ

If I am to live in the flesh, that means fruitful labor for me. Yet which I shall choose I cannot tell. I am hard pressed between the two. My desire is to depart and be with Christ, for that is far better. But to remain in the flesh is more necessary on your account. Convinced of this, I know that I will remain and continue with you all, for your progress and joy in the faith, so that in me you may have ample cause to glory in Christ Jesus, because of my coming to you again.

MEDITATE

As we've already seen, God's ultimate purpose for our remaining time here on earth is his glory in our progress in the two journeys: the internal journey of sanctification and the external journey of gospel advancement. Sanctification is clearly revealed as growth in conformity to Christ—our Christlikeness (see Rom 8:29). This sentiment shows how far Paul had progressed in conformity to Christ. Paul has been transformed by Christ in his view of life and death. His selflessness is astonishing, and to a degree, it reflects the perfect love Christ had for his people when he chose by his incarnation to leave the beauty, peace, and pleasures of his heavenly throne for our salvation. Because of his selfless love, it was better by far for Christ to come to earth, serve, suffer, and die than to remain in the perfect environs of heaven.

Though Paul is infinitely short of Christ in this regard, we can see the marks of conformity to Christ in him. Paul is wrestling with a simple question: Would you rather live or die? He is discussing his future: what will happen to him concerning his imprisonment. In the end, he will either be executed or released. In Philippians 1:21–26, he is wrestling not only with what he thinks would happen but also with what he would *like* to happen, what he would *prefer*.

Here are the options: he can go on living in the body, serving Christ and his people. Or he can die and go to heaven to experience his "gain" (1:21). The remarkable thing is that Paul sees nothing but advantages to both. No one suffered as much as Paul to spread the gospel of Christ (see 2 Cor 11), so Paul was well aware that more service would mean more suffering, even intense suffering. Yet going to heaven was for him personally "far better" (v. 24). It would mean seeing the full glories of Christ face to face, experiencing the perfect world free from death, mourning, crying, and pain (Rev 21:4). But remaining in this world would result in a more and more abundant harvest of fruit, and it would be "more necessary" for the Philippian Christians.

That settled it for Paul! In this argumentation, he is most like Christ. He would rather suffer more for the sake of the Philippians and all the other Christians he could win and train in the gospel than go to his heavenly reward.

REFLECT ON CHRIST

Paul's attitude here is very much an example of what he will call "the mind of Christ" (Phil 2:5; 1 Cor 2:16). Christ laid himself down for his people. He suffered for their blessedness. He died for their life. He did all this "for the joy that was set before him" (Heb 12:2). We see how Paul's desire to know Christ and be made like him, conformed to the "fellowship of his sufferings" (3:10 KJV), has resulted in the highest level of sanctification we can attain in this world. Christ led the way in this dying and rising, and his servant followed him. As well, Paul sets an example for us, saying, "follow me as I follow Christ."

In 2 Corinthians 8:9, Paul presents Jesus as the timeless example of Christian giving: "For you know the grace of our Lord Jesus Christ, that though he was rich, yet for your sake he became poor, so that you by his poverty might become rich." Paul will expound on this concept in the next chapter of Philippians. Christ left his throne of heavenly glory to give eternal blessings to us. Paul's mindset is so similar here. He is willing to forego his own heavenly blessedness for a time, so that by his suffering service he might make many rich. Certainly, he did this by his ministry of evangelism, but here the focus is on his ministry of intensive discipleship, helping the Philippians to make progress in their joy and faith in Christ Jesus.

APPLY GOD'S WORD

Every Christian should have an eternally fruitful ministry. As we've already said, we should be living for the two journeys of sanctification and gospel advance. The key to the harvest of fruit is the willingness to die to yourself for the spiritual benefits that will come to others.

Ask God to give you this kind of servant heart. Seek opportunities to suffer so that others may be blessed. Find ways that your selfless service may result in growth and abundant joy in Christ for others (vv. 25–26). We are all naturally selfish. It is very hard for us to learn to die so that others may live. But the joys of heavenly reward should move us to this kind of sacrificial living. Live such a fruitful life and develop such a rich meditation on heaven that you would actually be torn between the two!

PRAY

God would you please work both of these in me. Would you teach me what it means to live in Christ and for Christ at every moment? Would you help me to live for the heavenly reward of seeing seeds I planted with much labor and tears come to eternal fruition? Amen.

STUDY IT FURTHER

1. Read 2 Corinthians 11:23–28. What do these verses teach you about Paul's level of suffering? How do they make his statement, "I am torn between the two," here in Philippians 1 so amazing? Life for Paul was hard, vicious, and extreme. Yet Paul was willing to delay his arrival in heaven, suffering more persecution on earth for the benefit of others. How does his example inspire you?

2. In Colossians 3:1–4, Paul urges Christians to set their minds on things above and things to come. Why is heaven-mindedness such a good thing in the Christian life? How would it help you to focus more on the glories of heaven? How would it inspire you to serve more here on earth?

3. Find a copy of my book on heaven, *The Glory Now Revealed: What We'll Discover About God in Heaven*. Read the chapter on rewards. Let those meditations strengthen your zeal to live maximally on earth for heavenly glories.

Day 11

Philippians 1:27–30

READ

Only let your manner of life be worthy of the gospel of Christ, so that whether I come and see you or am absent, I may hear of you that you are standing firm in one spirit, with one mind striving side by side for the faith of the gospel, and not frightened in anything by your opponents. This is a clear sign to them of their destruction, but of your salvation, and that from God. For it has been granted to you that for the sake of Christ you should not only believe in him but also suffer for his sake, engaged in the same conflict that you saw I had and now hear that I still have.

MEDITATE

The church at Philippi was born through tribulation, and it seemed that it could only grow the same way. Paul and Silas were unjustly beaten and imprisoned, with their feet fastened in stocks at the center of the nasty, dark jail. Though the power of God was on display in the subsequent earthquake, and even more in the gospel work done in the hearts of the Philippian jailer and his family, a hot coalbed of persecution was still hissing with trouble for the newborn church at Philippi, and Paul knew it well. He says the Philippians were "engaged in the same conflict that you saw I had [i.e., in Philippi] and now hear that I still have [i.e., Paul's present imprisonment]." Paul knew it was vital for this young church to stand firm in the midst of this Satanic assault of persecution. He knew Christ's parable of the seed and the soils; the stony-ground hearers are characterized by an initial reception of the word with joy, but when trouble or persecution comes because of the word, they quickly fall away (Mark 4:17). Paul knew that now was their time of testing, and it was vital for them to let their "manner of life be worthy of the gospel of Christ." The gospel has the power to liberate all true believers from fear of death and suffering, as Paul had clearly demonstrated. Paul called on these young Philippian believers to stand "firm in one spirit, with one mind striving side by side for the faith of the gospel, and not frightened in anything by [their] opponents" (1:27–28). The fearless boldness of the early Christian church was one of the most powerful evidences of the truth of the gospel of Christ's resurrection that they preached. It would eventually result in the spiritual conquest of the mighty Roman Empire.

This supernatural calm, this utter fearlessness in the face of death, was a clear sign from God—a sign of the ultimate perdition of God's enemies and the ultimate salvation of his people. Paul and Silas singing in the Philippian jail was an example of this fearlessness, which led the jailer to ask the key question, "What must I do to be saved?" (Acts 16:30), or in other words, "How can I overcome my fear of death?"

Paul uses this language concerning the suffering of the Philippians: "It has been granted to you that for the sake of Christ you should not only believe in him but also suffer for his sake" (Phil 1:29). He says it is granted to them, like a gift from the King. And so it is! Christ said, "Blessed are you when they revile and persecute you and say all kinds of evil against you falsely for my sake. Rejoice and be exceedingly glad, for great is your reward in heaven!" (Matt 5:11–12 NKJV). If the Philippians could pass this test, surviving the onslaught, they would have clear assurance in their own hearts of their salvation, as well as eternal rewards in heaven. And for some of their persecutors, the result might be their own conversion, as happened so many years before with Saul of Tarsus.

REFLECT ON CHRIST

Christ's calling on his disciples is immeasurably high. He calls them to suffering and (possibly) even to death for his name. He led the way as the first grain of wheat that fell into the earth and died, resulting in a vast harvest of fruit (John 12:24). What he himself did, he now empowers his followers to do by his Spirit. Jesus is a mighty King, boldly commanding the highest level of allegiance in his followers, having already walked the same path himself.

As we consider this passage, we must do so only in the light of Christ. He is a meek and lowly Savior, not crushing his people with burdens they cannot carry. Fill your mind and heart with Christ now. Be willing to bow your neck and take his yoke upon you, for his yoke is indeed easy and his burden is light. How can this be? Because by his Spirit, he stoops under the weight to carry it with you. Ponder the words, "It has been granted to you that for the sake of Christ you should not only believe in him but also suffer for his sake." Ask him to make you worthy of this immeasurably high calling.

APPLY GOD'S WORD

The text calls us to let our conduct be worthy of the gospel of Christ. What does that mean? Narrowly in this one passage, it means courageously suffering persecution for the gospel if he calls you to that. In our context, very few of us have to face imprisonment or beatings for our Christian faith (although that may well change in our lifetime and certainly in the lifetimes of our children and grandchildren). But more applicably perhaps, our conduct in all respects must line up with the gospel of Christ: our thoughts, our words, our daily actions, our marriages, our parenting, our church involvement, the way we work, the way we manage our money and possessions. Ask the Spirit to search you and show you if your conduct really is worthy of the gospel of Christ.

Additionally, ask the Lord to make you increasingly willing to be persecuted for righteousness' sake. It may not be directly for your Christian faith, but it could be for your views on the sanctity of human life from conception, or on the sacredness of marriage as a covenant union between one man and one woman for life, or on sexual purity, or on justice issues, or on any one of a number of biblical values that are presently under attack. Stand firm in the faith and don't give way to fear.

PRAY

Heavenly Father, you have called us to stand with Christ "outside the camp and bear the reproach he endured" (Heb 13:13). Strengthen me in that calling for your kingdom's sake and for the salvation of those who would persecute me. Amen.

STUDY IT FURTHER

1. Read Hebrews 11:32–40. Those verses depict the sufferings of great men and women of faith from the Old Testament era. How has the church continued to suffer in the two thousand years since Christ's resurrection? Why is boldness and fearlessness in suffering and death so vital to our witness?

2. Read the account of the martyrdom of Stephen in Acts 7. How do you think Stephen's courage and sweetness in death may have made a lasting impression on Saul (Paul)?

3. What does this passage in Philippians 1 teach you about faith? What does it teach you about the cost of the spread of the gospel? Tertullian once said (during the era of the Roman persecution of the church), "The blood of martyrs is seed." How is that true? How did Paul's doctrine here point in that direction?

Day 12

Philippians 2:1–4

READ

So if there is any encouragement in Christ, any comfort from love, any participation in the Spirit, any affection and sympathy, complete my joy by being of the same mind, having the same love, being in full accord and of one mind. Do nothing from selfish ambition or conceit, but in humility count others more significant than yourselves. Let each of you look not only to his own interests, but also to the interests of others.

MEDITATE

The entrance of sin into the world through Adam's rebellion has had the effect of a grenade, blasting apart the things that God created to be together. First and foremost, Adam and Eve's relationship with God died at that instant—each became spiritually dead in their transgressions even while they lived physically (Eph 2:1). Second, Adam's relationship of true oneness with Eve was severed—they were ashamed and hid from each other. Third, Adam and Eve's relationship with creation was cursed—the ground would now wrestle against Adam every season, Eve would bear children in pain, and eventually the earth would claim their corpses at the end of their lives.

By contrast, God's work of redemption is to reunite all things under the headship of Christ so that "God may be all in all" (1 Cor 15:28). The eternal oneness the redeemed will experience in heaven is patterned after the perfect unity of the Trinity, as Jesus prayed, "That they may be one, even as we are one" (John 17:11, 22). Imagine this: for all eternity, a countless multitude of the redeemed from every nation and culture and language on earth (Rev 7:9) will be as perfectly one as God the Father, the Son, and the Spirit are one.

What is the nature of that perfect oneness? These practical exhortations to the Philippian Christians give us some idea. Look at verse 2: "being of the same mind, having the same love, being in full accord and of one mind." Let's break down each of these points. First, the first and the last of these four commands is the same in the Greek—"like-minded," thinking the exact same way. About what? Honestly and amazingly, about everything. The Father, the Son, and the Spirit are one in mind about every atom in the universe and every moment in history; they have been from before the foundation of the world and will be through all eternity. There has never been the slightest disagreement in the godhead about anything, and there never will be. Second, the oneness of the Trinity means they have "the same love." As we discussed a few days ago, love can be likened to a magnetic attraction and hatred to a magnetic repulsion. God loves some things (e.g., his creation, his glory, righteousness, his people, etc.) and hates other things (e.g., wickedness and idolatry). God doesn't love and hate various things to the same degree; God loves/hates some things more than others. For example, the angel appearing to Daniel says he is "a man greatly loved" (Dan 10:11). Amazingly, the Trinity loves and hates all things in complete agreement; there is not the slightest difference in degree of love between the Father, the Son, or the Spirit concerning any topic in the universe. Third, the Father, the Son, and the Spirit are "in full accord," meaning they have the same purpose and are equally engaged in bringing it about. The Greek literally means "one soul." These four concepts give us a priceless glimpse into the unity of the godhead.

This oneness is exactly how Paul wants the Philippians to be with each other. The New Testament exhorts Christians to moral action by saying, "This is what you are, and this is what you will be in heaven, so now move toward that." They should be truly one spiritually with other Christians. They will spend eternity in perfect oneness—same mind, same love, same purpose. So, they should live like it right now, every day. Negatively, this means they should do nothing through the selfish ambition or prideful conceit that characterizes non-Christians. Rather, considering others better than themselves and others' interests more important than their own, they should live as servants of each other.

REFLECT ON CHRIST

Paul's beautiful exhortations toward oneness are rooted in their relationship with Christ. First, they are *in Christ*—that is, spiritually united with him. From this, they have received "comfort" (the Greek word is related to the word "comforter" assigned to the Holy Spirit, a rich word of help, exhortation, wisdom, advice, and consolation from sadness) in Christ from his unconditional love for them, from fellowship with one another through the Spirit, from affection for one another and mercy toward one another. These virtues and many others are fully available to them as Christians. All of them flow from being in Christ as members of one body. The Spirit of Christ is in them, powerfully working the beautiful exhortations of perfect unity (v. 2) in them all.

As we will see tomorrow, the mindset of Christ's lowliness is also ours in Christ—the ability to think of others more than ourselves. Christ's staggering example of humility, of leaving heavenly glory and going to the cross, is the foundation of Paul's appeal to the Philippians to stop being selfish and disagreeing and arguing with each other as they were doing (2:14; 4:2–3).

APPLY GOD'S WORD

The application for this text flows right from the commands of verses 2–4. God the Holy Spirit wants all Christians to live in perfect unity with each other here on earth. To that end, we must meditate on the perfect unity of the godhead as Jesus prays in John 17 and as is described in verse 2. Then we should acknowledge our sinful pride and selfishness as described clearly in verses 3–4. We are often motivated by selfish ambition and prideful conceit, and our pride tends to make us think we are better than others, leading us to pursue our own agendas constantly. After confessing these continual tendencies of the flesh, we should ask the Holy Spirit to kill these sinful attitudes and the selfish actions that flow from them. We must obey these commands daily, looking for specific ways in our marriages, our family lives, our church relationships, and even in the world to carry out Paul's clear commands here. We should pray continually, "Lord, you served me at the cross; now let me serve others today."

PRAY

Father, you exist in perfect oneness at every moment with the Son and the Spirit. Because of my sin, I was severed from oneness with you and with others. Thanks be to God, I have been redeemed! Give me power by the Spirit to kill my pride, selfishness, and personal agendas. Make me a servant, as humble as Jesus was. Amen.

STUDY IT FURTHER

1. Read John 17:11 and John 17:23. What does it mean for Christians to be one as the Father and the Son are one? Read Galatians 3:28, where it says we are all one in Christ. How do these verses in Philippians 2:4–5 give us a sense of the perfect oneness we should experience on earth?

2. Read Ephesians 1:10. What is God's ultimate plan for the oneness of the universe in Christ?

3. How does sin destroy that oneness? How have you seen disunity in your life? Your family? Your church? Your community? Your nation? Your world? How do you picture perfect oneness in heaven?

Day 13

Philippians 2:5–8

READ

Have this mind among yourselves, which is yours in Christ Jesus, who, though he was in the form of God, did not count equality with God a thing to be grasped, but emptied himself, by taking the form of a servant, being born in the likeness of men. And being found in human form, he humbled himself by becoming obedient to the point of death, even death on a cross.

MEDITATE AND REFLECT ON CHRIST

There is no mystery in the Christian faith greater than the incarnation of the Son of God. The second-century defender of the doctrine of Christ's full deity and humanity, Athanasius, likened the infinite depths of Christ to observing wave upon wave of the ocean rolling endlessly upon the shore. Our minds can scarcely take in the dimensions of one aspect of Christ's infinite person before another aspect comes rolling upon us. Paul himself said that in Christ are "hidden all the treasures of wisdom and knowledge" (Col 2:3). All of them! How then can finite minds like ours take in that fullness? Since even in heaven we will not be omniscient, it will be our pleasure to keep learning new aspects of Christ for all eternity.

Here Paul focuses on the "mind of Christ Jesus," his attitude of humility. In verses 6–8, he traces out the downward journey on which Christ's humility took him—from the heavenly glory of equality with God to the shame and condemnation of the cross as our sin-bearer. Paul asserts the full equality of the pre-incarnate Christ with God, and he also asserts that Christ did not consider it robbery to be seen as equal with God. God's throne was his throne; God's glory was his glory. In John 17:5, Jesus prays for the Father to glorify him with the glory Jesus had with him before the world existed. Only if Jesus were fully God would such a request not be seen as blasphemous, for God has asserted plainly, "My glory I will not give to another" (Isa 48:11). Glory is the radiant display of the perfections (attributes) of God. Jesus emptied himself of that radiant display and the full exercise of those attributes by choosing to take upon himself the form of a bondservant, coming in the likeness of humans. He made himself lowly and lived a whole life in the pattern of this perfect humility. At every moment, he lived as a servant—a servant of God and a servant of man. In every word, in every work, Jesus only did the will of his Father. This pattern of perfect, humble obedience took him to the infinite depths of crucifixion under the wrath of God at Calvary.

It boggles the mind that Christ was every bit as much a servant as he was God. Paul says in verse 6 that Christ was "in the form of God," and then in verse 7, he took on "the form of a servant." Christ was not merely acting as a servant—he truly *was* a servant. Sometimes we take on temporary roles as children do in a school play, wearing a costume and acting like a servant. Christ did not do this. To the deepest part of his being as a man, he considered himself a servant of God and of others. This servant mind continued in Jesus all his earthly life in a downward journey of humiliation. His mission was utterly perplexing to the Jewish nation, including his own disciples. And when he willingly obeyed his Father in Gethsemane and went with his enemies to die, his disciples deserted him and fled. The Jewish population screamed for his death, probably because the humiliation of the triumphant Son of David was more than they could bear. His enemies spat upon him and abused him both physically and verbally, then exulted over him while he was dying, mocking him with savage tongues. Even then, Jesus never ceased to be God. At any moment he could have risen up and crushed his abusers, but his obedience to his Father went all the way to death.

The more we meditate on Christ's humility, the more the "mind of Christ" is worked in us and the more shameful our pride, selfish ambitions, and selfish agendas become. This meditation has the power to work continual repentance in us, causing us to turn away from the "mind of the flesh" to the "mind of the Spirit" (Rom 8:6–7), which is the mind of Christ. This work is not easy, for the roots of our sinful pride go deep into our hearts.

APPLY GOD'S WORD

Paul's soaring theological insights are very practical—that the Philippians would humble themselves and treat each other with loving sacrificial service. The Spirit is pressing the command of verse 5 onto every Christian with the earlier commands of verses 2–4 in view. We are commanded to have the same mind in us which was in Christ. Every regenerate person already has the mind of Christ (1 Cor 2:16), but effectively Philippians 2:5–8 is telling us to *use* it. We are called on to take up our cross and follow Jesus downward in humility, slaughtering our pride and selfishness so that we may serve others.

This life of humble service will be displayed in countless ways in our lives. It will cause us to seek to understand the perspectives and needs of others and to act on their behalf as if their cause were our own. It will cause us to stop interrupting others, to stop arguing, and to use our time, energy, and money to benefit others rather than ourselves. It will propel us to evangelize and to alleviate suffering through mercy ministries. For a chosen few, it will result in literal martyrdom for the gospel.

Our liberation from pride will be finally consummated in heaven. We will be perfectly humble and will genuinely consider the life stories of our brothers and sisters as enthralling, their glory as greater than our own, their rewards as genuinely deserved. This chapter calls on us to think that way now and live accordingly.

PRAY

Father, we are in awe of your Son. His downward journey of suffering servanthood is the life path of all Christians, and this passage calls us to follow it. Give us strength for that immeasurable descent. Help us to slaughter our pride, our selfish ambitions, and our selfish works to your glory. Amen.

STUDY IT FURTHER

1. Read the account of Jesus's suffering prayer in Gethsemane (Mark 14:32–36; Luke 22:39–44). How does that account help us understand the incredible humility and suffering involved in Jesus's decision to go to the cross? How does that inspire us to humility in servanthood in our lives?

2. Read Isaiah 14:12–15 and Ezekiel 28:13–17. Those passages describe the fall of Satan before the creation of the world. The essence of his fall was that Satan was filled with soaring ambition and pride that led him to try to take God's place. How is human sin similar to Satan's? How does the example of Christ in Philippians 2 help to conquer our own soaring, devilish pride?

3. Read a summary of the life of Amy Carmichael. She was an Irish missionary who spent her whole adult life in India caring for orphaned girls. How could studying such an example of suffering servanthood motivate you?

Day 14

Philippians 2:9–11

READ

Therefore God has highly exalted him and bestowed on him the name that is above every name, so that at the name of Jesus every knee should bow, in heaven and on earth and under the earth, and every tongue confess that Jesus Christ is Lord, to the glory of God the Father.

MEDITATE AND REFLECT ON CHRIST

The word "therefore" in verse 9 represents God's righteous reward of his Son's perfect and total obedience. We see a V-shaped journey for Jesus, from heavenly glory to earthly humility in his birth, continued downward through many steps of humble service in obedience to the will of the Father, even to death on the cross. This was as low as Christ could go, deeper than the deepest trench in the ocean floor. But because Christ did all this in humble obedience to the will of the Father, God would not leave him there. "Therefore" means it was right for God to exalt Jesus highly, and it will also be right (at a much lower level) for God to exalt any who follow Christ in humble service to the people of God. As Jesus said in John 12:26, "If anyone serves me, he must follow me; and where I am, there will my servant be also. If anyone serves me, the Father will honor him."

Again, we feel the weight of Paul's commands to all Christians to be humble servants of others, to consider others as better than ourselves and the needs of others as more important than our own. Christ in his incarnation is our pattern in this. We have briefly probed Christ's downward journey from heavenly glory to the humiliation of the cross and the Father's righteous response: "Therefore God has highly exalted him." This exaltation is essential for us to comprehend, for the selfishness of the flesh thinks only of what we will lose if we live in humble service to others. God intends that we understand Christ's exaltation as a cause for worship but also as motivation and promise for us.

But the exaltation of even the choicest servant of God will still be far below that of Christ. God highly exalted his obedient Son to the *highest place* by giving him the "name that is above every name." And what name is that? The name of God. The Father would never share his name with a creature, but it is right for him to share it with his Son. It says that at the name of Jesus, "every knee should bow" in heaven, on earth, and under the earth. This is a quotation of Isaiah 45:23 in which Almighty God swears by himself that before him every knee shall bow and every tongue take its oath. The context in Isaiah 45 is of God's contest with the gods of the nations that had stolen the hearts of his people. God proclaims plainly in Isaiah 40–49 that there is no God but him. This is the exact phrase Paul uses to speak of God's exaltation of his Son. If Jesus were not God, such an ascription would be blasphemous. Instead, it is prophetic; in the future, every creature in the universe will fall before the glory of Jesus, and they will confess, "Jesus is Lord." This means he is a deity, worthy of full worship. And all the glory and worship that flows from the hearts and lips of the people to Jesus goes ultimately to God the Father, for anyone who says that "Jesus is Lord" is saying so "to the glory of God the Father."

APPLY GOD'S WORD

We should be in awe at the sacrifice of Jesus, who left his heavenly throne of glory and traveled downward in total obedience to his Father for our sakes. First, as we are moved deeply by these words, let us worship Jesus. Let us boast in him, speak of him, sing to him, praise him, love him. We were created for this and redeemed for this, and we will spend eternity worshiping him. Let's start now, falling before him in his exalted status as the Son of God.

Second, let us have the "mind of Christ" in obedience to God. It was one man's disobedience that brought sin into the world, and it was one man's obedience that brought salvation (Rom 5:19). All sin is rebellion, disobedience to Almighty God. Christ's mind was only to obey God, no matter what it cost him. This passage is meant to make us as obedient as he was, to be willing to die to ourselves for the benefit of others.

Third, let us keep in mind the overall purpose of Philippians 2:1–11—to bring all Christians to perfect unity and make us humble, self-denying servants of each other, considering others as better than ourselves. We should seek practical ways to live this out.

Finally, let us bask in the promise of future reward that Christ has made to all who will follow him and serve others. The Father will honor all who travel the same downward journey of costly self-denial in service to others (John 12:24–26).

PRAY

Father, we confess that the humbling work in us has a long way to go. Please finish that work in us by the example of Jesus and the power of the Spirit. Let it all flow from hearts of passionate worship of Christ, as our tongues cry out, "Jesus is Lord, to the glory of God the Father!" Amen.

STUDY IT FURTHER

1. Read Matthew 23:12. There Jesus says, "Whoever exalts himself will be humbled, and whoever humbles himself will be exalted." How does that verse partner with Philippians 2:5–11? How can we practically "humble ourselves"? What would happen if we started praying every day, "Lord, humble me deeply and profoundly today"? Would you be scared to pray that prayer?

2. Read in Daniel 4 about how God humbled the arrogant tyrant Nebuchadnezzar. What was the final lesson he learned as he wrote his account? Would you consider that final lesson, "those who walk in pride he [God] is able to humble," a warning or a promise?

3. All of the redeemed will be radiantly glorious in heaven, for Jesus said, "Then the righteous will shine like the sun in the kingdom of their Father" (Matt 13:43). How will we be both perfectly beautiful and perfectly humble?

Day 15

Philippians 2:12

READ

Therefore, my beloved, as you have always obeyed, so now, not only as in my presence but much more in my absence, work out your own salvation with fear and trembling ...

MEDITATE

Today we come to the paradox of the relationship between human effort ("work out your salvation") and divine power ("for it is God who works in you," 2:13) in our salvation. Many Christians have sought to resolve this by emphasizing too much of one side and minimizing the other. Some say our salvation is achieved by passively relying on God to do everything—"Let go and let God." Others go to the opposite extreme, saying everything depends on us—strict patterns of spiritual disciplines and zealous rules of holiness without which we will be lost. Neither of these extremes is biblical Christianity.

Scripture teaches us that our salvation comes in stages, and the rules of engagement are different for each of those stages. In justification, all our sins (past, present, and future) are 100 percent forgiven by grace through faith in Christ alone, with no works on our part required or welcomed by God. The thief on the cross is a perfect picture of this—he trusted in Christ alone and could do no works at all to earn his forgiveness. After justification, we are commanded to begin the "internal journey" of sanctification. The rules of engagement for the sanctification journey are different than those for justification, for our energetic works are essential to our progress toward Christian maturity. Yet, we are instructed that even then our works are initiated by the commands of God's word and energized by the power of God's Spirit working within us. There is no passage better than Philippians 2:12–13 for teaching this mysterious partnership of our work and God's work within us to achieve Christlikeness.

Before Paul ascended to the mountaintop of meditation on the humiliation and exaltation of Christ (2:5–11), he exhorted the Philippians to imitate Christ in humble service to each other (2:1–4). Verses 12–13 then extend to every area of their salvation, not just their humble service to each other. Paul wants them to obey in every area of their lives all the time. He urges them to work out their own salvation "with fear and trembling."

God is commanding all Christians for all time to make progress in sanctification by whatever efforts they can possibly exert. Christians must work at growing—work hard. The Christian life is portrayed in other places like a marathon in which we must discipline our bodies and bring them into subjection (1 Cor 9:27). We must lay aside every weight and the sin that so easily entangles us and run with endurance (Heb 12:1). Here, we are to work out our salvation "with fear and trembling." What does that mean? In this strong exhortation we should not forget that (1) we are completely forgiven at every moment simply by faith in Christ, never by any works; and (2) we are not working alone, but God is working in us every moment (more on that tomorrow). The "fear and trembling" is not terror of a God whose tyranny drives us to constant efforts to please him. Rather, it is a sense of the danger of sin and the pure fear of the Lord that would come upon us if we were to see God in his radiant holiness. Fearful of what sin can do to destroy our lives, we work out our salvation. And believing that a revelation of God's radiant light would drop us immediately to our knees, we work out our salvation.

REFLECT ON CHRIST

As we work out our own salvation with fear and trembling, we know that only by faith in Christ can we make a single step of progress. Paul rebuked the Galatians for thinking that they began the Christian life by faith in Christ but were then perfected by self-effort (Gal 3:3). In giving us the image of a marathon run with extreme endurance, the author to the Hebrews said they must run every step by "looking to Jesus, the founder and perfecter of our faith" (Heb 12:2). This work of growing in our salvation is the hardest thing we will ever do, but Christ has said plainly that he would not leave us as orphans (John 14:18). As we face the immense challenges of living a life of holiness, our first thought must always be of Christ Jesus, crucified and resurrected. By his death we are completely forgiven, and by his resurrection we have the power of a new life within us by the indwelling Spirit.

APPLY GOD'S WORD

The possible applications of today's passage are as deep as the commands of God and as wide as the circumstances in which all of God's people will find themselves today. God demands continual obedience to all of his commands but that obedience is something we can only achieve by his power which works within us. In humility, we must learn to say to Christ, "You are the vine; I am the branch. Apart from you, I can do nothing today." Then we must get specific in our prayer time with the Lord: "What do you want me to do today for my own holiness and your glory? What sin do I need to slay by the Spirit? What costly service do you want me to render to another person today? How can I make vigorous progress today for your glory and the advance of Christ's kingdom?" Then whatever the Lord by his Spirit says to you, go and do it with fear and trembling—but also with joy, knowing that God gives you the power you need to do it all.

PRAY

Lord, these verses search us and try us to the core of our being. Please give us boldness to stand under these words and allow them to transform our lives. Please help us to hold in healthy tension our own work and your work in us so that we can grow more and more into Christlikeness. Amen.

STUDY IT FURTHER

1. How is the issue of God's sovereignty and human effort in salvation addressed here? How do you understand the combination of God's work in us and our work on ourselves? How do the following verses add to our understanding of this issue: 1 Corinthians 15:9–10; Romans 8:13–14; Ezekiel 2:1–2? Why is it vital for us to understand this issue properly?

2. What do you think God is telling you to do to work out your own salvation? What are some sins that are besetting you and causing you particular trouble? How could the

power of the Holy Spirit be at work in you to kill those sins (Rom 8:13–14)?

3. What would happen if you overemphasized either God's work in us or our need to work?

Day 16

Philippians 2:13

READ

... for it is God who works in you, both to will and to work for his good pleasure.

MEDITATE

The command for us to work out our own salvation with fear and trembling may be overwhelming at times. As we saw in the previous passage, there is no doubt that we must take full responsibility for making progress toward Christlike perfection. We can never relent for a moment, for sin will seize that opportunity and work deadly consequences in our lives. A large part of the "fear and trembling" is knowing what sin can do.

But the centerpiece of "fear and trembling" is the majestic person of Almighty God, by whose power all things exist. Paul wants us to know that the ultimate power source for our growth in our salvation is God. How can we possibly comprehend the dimensions of God's power, for he is omnipotent? There is nothing his power cannot do. He created the entire universe in six days "by the word of his power" (Heb 1:3). From that moment until this, God has sustained every atom in the universe by his power as well. This mighty God has determined to save every one of the elect, not merely beginning their salvation but completing it. As we saw in Philippians 1:6, God began a good work (salvation) in our souls and will keep working at it until it is complete. Today's passage is teaching the same thing, but it goes beyond this by saying *how* God's power is working to finish our salvation. God is working in us at every moment "both to will and to work for his good pleasure." God has mysterious access to the very core of our being, and he is able to shape our hearts so that we love what he loves and hate what he hates. The heart's inclination of loving or hating is the very framework out of which we make all our choices, by which we "will and work." Many people speak of "free will," as though a human will is unfettered to anything at all, but we always make choices based on the affections of our hearts, and God has the power to work in our hearts to cause us to love what is good and hate what is evil.

This limitless power of God at work in our lives is completely tied to his good pleasure, for God himself loves what is pure and beautiful and glorious. God is skillfully and relentlessly working in all his children every single day to move them along the path of righteousness to final conformity to Christ. God wants us to work hard on our souls but to do so at every moment knowing that he is working in us as well, and he cannot be defeated; what he has purposed, he will do.

Today's text is both a relentless command for us to be holy as Christ is holy, and at the same time a limitless fountain of encouragement to focus our minds on the power of God mysteriously at work within us. We are not on our own. Almighty God is focusing his power on our final salvation.

REFLECT ON CHRIST

The "good pleasure" of God is to make us all like Christ. Every thought of our minds, every motion of our hearts, every action of our bodies should be conformed to the perfection of Christ. The powerful working of God in us is always toward that end. Therefore, in Ephesians 1:19, Paul prays for us to realize that the "exceeding greatness of his power" at work in us believers is the same power that raised Jesus Christ from the dead. Whenever we may be tempted to get discouraged at the progress we are making in our sanctification, let us learn to meditate on the power of God in raising Christ from the dead and exalting him to his own right hand in heaven. Let us realize that nothing is too difficult for our omnipotent God.

Let us move out in faith today, following in Christ's footsteps of humble servanthood, seeking to obey the will of God at every moment. Christ said, "I always do what pleases him" (John 8:29). The Spirit of Christ is within us working the same attitude of glad obedience. When we are complete, we will no longer live for selfish interests but for the interests of God and of others.

APPLY GOD'S WORD

Begin today by meditating on the infinite power of God in creation. Think of what God did by speaking into existence vast galaxies in outer space, as well as intricately interconnected ecosystems of life here on Earth. Think also of the power he displayed in Christ's birth, miraculous life, atoning death, powerful resurrection, and ascension to his own right hand in heaven. Say to yourself, "This powerful God is working in my soul today to will and to do according to his good pleasure." Then search the Scriptures to determine what specific course of service he would have you do today. Finally, ask him to lead you by his Holy Spirit to do what he wants you to do today. Our flesh demands that we meet our own needs and desires. The Spirit of Christ demands a life of self-denial and sacrifice for his glory. Philippians 2:12–13 teaches you how to make the right choice.

PRAY

Almighty God, Creator of the ends of the earth, your power is limitless. This passage teaches me that you are powerfully at work in my soul, moving me both to will and to work according to your good pleasure. Please, Lord, do it all the more. Amen.

STUDY IT FURTHER

1. To increase your sense of "fear and trembling" at the holiness of God, study the following passages: Isaiah 6:1–5; Ezekiel 1:28; 3:23; 9:8; 11:13; 43:3; 44:4; Matthew 17:6; Revelation 1:17. All these passages show the reaction of sinners to the holy presence of God. How does meditating on these passages help you grow in a healthy fear of sin and of the holiness of God?

2. Someone once said, "Sin always takes you farther than you want to go, keeps you longer than you want to stay, and costs more than you want to pay." How does that saying help you grow in your fear of the effects of sin in your life?

3. How does the fact that God's omnipotence is at work in you to grow you from the inside in holiness give you confidence in your Christian life? How does Ezekiel 36:27 relate to this statement that God is at work in you "to will and to work according to his good pleasure"?

Day 17

Philippians 2:14–18

READ

Do all things without grumbling or disputing, that you may be blameless and innocent, children of God without blemish in the midst of a crooked and twisted generation, among whom you shine as lights in the world, holding fast to the word of life, so that in the day of Christ I may be proud that I did not run in vain or labor in vain. Even if I am to be poured out as a drink offering upon the sacrificial offering of your faith, I am glad and rejoice with you all. Likewise you also should be glad and rejoice with me.

MEDITATE

Sin has made this world a dark place. The darkness of human depravity is evident here, for Paul speaks of the Philippians as living among a "crooked and twisted generation." But Paul likens Christians to stars shining in a dark night sky (the Greek word *phōstēr*, "lights," is often translated "stars"). When Jesus entered the world, he fulfilled the wonderful prophecy of Isaiah 9:2, "The people who walked in darkness have seen a great light." Jesus claimed, "I am the light of the world" (John

8:12). Amazingly, he also said to his disciples, "You are the light of the world" (Matt 5:14). The most vital way that Christians are called to shine in this darkness is by "holding fast to the word of life," which is the gospel. The word translated "holding fast" can also be translated as "holding forth." Both are vital: as we hold fast to the gospel ourselves, we are transformed by it; then we can hold forth the gospel through bold proclamation of it to the lost.

But if we are corrupted by sin ourselves, if we are every bit as selfish and greedy and angry and prideful as lost people, we will not shine at all. It would be as though we have hidden our light under a basket, as Jesus said in Matthew 5:15. This lofty call to bold and clear witness in our dark world becomes as practical as killing the sins of grumbling and arguing. Paul begins this section by giving this command in the name of the Lord. Only if we obey and put these sins to death will we be "blameless and innocent, children of God without blemish."

Complaining and arguing are so commonplace in human experience that we may well wonder why God cares about them. But he does. They are actually very great sins, though we may not think so. Complaining flows from the great corruption of not trusting the providence of God in your life and failing to praise and thank God at all times for all things. We complain about the weather, our aches and pains, our family members, our governmental leaders, our bosses, our financial situation, almost everything that displeases us in some way. We were created and redeemed to praise God, and when we complain, we are doing the exact opposite. Thus, we are like sinful Israel during the time of the exodus who murmured against God constantly, complaining about the pursuing Egyptian army, the lack of water to drink, the lack of food to eat, the constant supply of manna rather than meat, and the challenges of conquering the promised land. God was very angry with them and at one point sent poisonous serpents to kill many of them for their complaining (Num 21:6). Arguing is just as bad as complaining. We bicker, quarrel, and dispute with our spouses, our children, our neighbors, our coworkers, our fellow church members—with just about everyone. These arguments flow from the same selfishness and pride that Paul wrote against in Philippians 2:3–4.

The call here is very high. We are to be so filled with trust for the providence of God that we submit gladly and peacefully to whatever he ordains for our lives. That will kill all complaining. We are also to be so filled with humble love for others that we gladly listen to their needs and perspective and stop arguing with them. This work of deep humility resulting in continual servant hearts will glow with the light of the gospel in this present dark age.

REFLECT ON CHRIST

The humble servanthood that enables us to stop complaining and arguing was perfectly displayed by Jesus Christ, as we've already seen in this chapter (2:5–11). Christ never complained against his persecutors, though they hated him "without a cause" (John 15:25). Christ never complained against the will of his Father, though it cost him his life. Christ certainly disputed many times with his enemies over the truths of God's word and of his own mission, but his arguments with them were never based on pride or selfishness. And when the time came for him to be put on trial, and many false witnesses rose up against him and unjustly accused him of things he never did, he never opened his mouth but entrusted himself to God who judges righteously (1 Pet 2:23). Christ is truly the light of the world, and as we follow him now by his Spirit, we will be empowered to shine in our generation as he did.

APPLY GOD'S WORD

The commands here are simple: stop complaining, stop arguing. It is not as though we don't understand these words—we do. However, we might think these sins are so commonplace that God will give us a pass on them. But God created and redeemed us in Christ to praise and thank him continually. Ask God to work deep repentance in you over your complaining and arguing. Ask him to reveal instances of complaining today throughout the day: while you're driving, or at work, or doing errands, or just having a conversation with a friend. When he does, immediately repent and ask God to kill the complaining spirit that assumes you deserve better than what God has willed for you today. And do the same with arguing. If you are married, ask your spouse to work with you in your marriage to obey this command. Ask the Spirit to give you a humble heart toward all other people, especially when they may disagree with you about anything at all.

Finally, ask God to do these things in you so that you can shine like a star in this dark world we are called to reach. It may be that, over time, these sins will be so subdued in your life that someone will ask you why you are so joyful and humble and peaceful all the time. Then you can hold forth the word of life for their salvation.

PRAY

Heavenly Father, teach me how much you hate these sins of complaining and arguing. Forgive me and transform me. Make me a humble servant in this twisted generation so that I can shine like a star and lead some out of darkness. Amen.

STUDY IT FURTHER

1. Read Exodus 17:1–7 and Psalm 95:7b–11. Why was God so angry at the complaining done by the Israelites?

2. What are some of the most common patterns of complaining you see in your life? How could the lessons of Christian contentment in Philippians 4:10–13 help you put this sin to death?

3. What does it mean to "shine as lights in the world" in this passage? How does it relate to our evangelism?

Day 18

Philippians 2:19–24

READ

I hope in the Lord Jesus to send Timothy to you soon, so that I too may be cheered by news of you. For I have no one like him, who will be genuinely concerned for your welfare. For they all seek their own interests, not those of Jesus Christ. But you know Timothy's proven worth, how as a son with a father he has served with me in the gospel. I hope therefore to send him just as soon as I see how it will go with me, and I trust in the Lord that shortly I myself will come also.

MEDITATE

What a high commendation the apostle Paul gives to his son in the faith, Timothy. Paul expresses the greatest level of confidence in Timothy as his messenger and coworker. Paul is in prison but continues to do everything he can to further the work of the gospel. Essential to that work is the planting of healthy churches who would multiply disciples in their region. Paul cannot continue to preach from place to place, but he is seeking to shepherd the churches he has already planted. Paul is continually concerned for those churches as he says plainly in 2 Corinthians 11:28–29: "Apart from other things, there is the daily pressure on me of my anxiety for all the churches. Who is weak, and I am not weak? Who is made to fall, and I am not indignant?" As a matter of fact, the pain Paul felt concerning churches being overwhelmed by persecution or sin may well have been greater than any of the physical sufferings he endured for Christ. Even in this chapter, he expresses his concern that he may have run or labored in vain with the Philippians (2:16). Since he is in prison, he is not able to visit the Philippian church, so he plans to send Timothy to them to find out how they are doing spiritually.

Paul writes this glowing recommendation of Timothy because he wanted to be sure the Philippians would receive Timothy with proper respect and accept any teaching and leadership he might give them. He says that Timothy is like-minded, seeing things the same way as his mentor Paul. Actually, Timothy is unusually like-minded, for Paul says there is "no one like him." Central to this was Timothy sharing Paul's deep concern for the state of the Philippians' spirituality. This is part of the transforming work of the gospel, to make us deeply care how others are doing spiritually. It is so different than the attitude of Cain who said, "Am I my brother's keeper?" (Gen 4:9). The work of the gospel calls us to be exactly this for one another—keepers for our spiritual brothers and sisters. We should care for them. The lost people of the world only care about selfish interests, Paul said. But Timothy had been so transformed by the gospel that all he cared about were the interests of Christ Jesus—the salvation of souls.

And this was not a fleeting fancy with Timothy but was his proven character. He had served side by side with Paul as a son does with his father. What a beautiful image that is. Think about the colonial days in America in which a son would apprentice under his father in the family trade—like Paul Revere learning the art of gold- and silversmithing from his father. Father and son worked side by side, and the father's heart would swell with pride and joy as the son learned the father's skills. So it was with Timothy in the work of the gospel.

Paul asserts that he will send Timothy to them when his own outcome is clear and he is convinced (as he said in chapter 1) that he himself will come soon.

REFLECT ON CHRIST

No earthly father has ever had greater delight in a son than our heavenly Father has over his only begotten Son, Jesus Christ. Twice in Jesus's life, the Father proclaimed this delight in an audible voice from heaven: "This is my beloved Son, with whom I am well pleased" (Matt 3:17; 17:5). Jesus himself spoke continually of his role as a Son working under his Father: "My Father is working until now, and I am working" (John 5:17); "The Son can do nothing of his own accord, but only what he sees the Father doing. For whatever the Father does, that the Son does likewise" (John 5:19). Jesus's submissive work went all the way to his perfect and final obedience to the Father's will at the cross and can be seen in every word he spoke in his life: "When you have lifted up the Son of Man, then you will know that I am he, and that I do nothing on my own authority, but speak just as the Father taught me" (John 8:28).

Since God is our Father as well, Jesus's comprehensive and glad submission to his Father in every work he did and every word he uttered is a powerful example for us. At a much lower level, we can find inspiration in Timothy as well, for he had learned from Paul to stop looking out for his own earthly interests and to look out for Christ's interests every single day.

APPLY GOD'S WORD

I find two applications here. First, in imitation of Timothy and ultimately of Christ, let us resolve to stop looking out for our own selfish worldly interests. Paul said that a selfish mindset is universal unless the Spirit transforms us and makes us live for Christ. Confess to God your tendencies to look out for your own selfish interests. Then ask him to move in you powerfully through the Spirit of sonship (Rom 8:15) to seek Christ's interests every single day. Ask the Spirit to show you how you spend your time, your energy, and your money. Is it for the kingdom or for yourself?

Second, for all of you parents, find inspiration in this passage to involve your children in works of ministry for the advancement of the kingdom of Christ. Teach them how the kids would apprentice in their father's trade to develop their skills. Tell them your ultimate family business is no physical trade but the spread of the kingdom of Christ through the ministry of the word. Inspire them to serve with you as Timothy did with Paul, as a son or daughter with their parent.

PRAY

O heavenly Father, you have adopted us into your family that we might serve your interests and not our own. We confess to you that we are selfish. Please forgive us and transform us. Make us like Timothy with his spiritual father, Paul. Teach us to look out for Christ's interests constantly. Amen.

STUDY IT FURTHER

1. Read all the quotes from the Gospel of John cited in today's devotional in their original context. What do they teach you about Christ's constant desire to please his Father? How can these verses help you grow in faithful service to Christ?

2. Why do you think we are tempted to look out for our own interests rather than those of Jesus Christ? Read 2 Corinthians 5:9–10. How can meditating on these two verses help sharpen our zeal for Christ's kingdom today?

3. Second Corinthians 5:9–10 also tells us we will have to give an account to Christ for everything we ever did in the body, whether good or bad. How does that accountability give you a healthy fear of the Lord and a desire to please him?

Day 19

Philippians 2:25–28

READ

I have thought it necessary to send to you Epaphroditus my brother and fellow worker and fellow soldier, and your messenger and minister to my need, for he has been longing for you all and has been distressed because you heard that he was ill. Indeed he was ill, near to death. But God had mercy on him, and not only on him but on me also, lest I should have sorrow upon sorrow. I am the more eager to send him, therefore, that you may rejoice at seeing him again, and that I may be less anxious.

MEDITATE

In this passage, Paul speaks of a man named Epaphroditus, whom he calls the Philippians' messenger who ministered to Paul's needs. We will spend two days understanding him and honoring him. We will also see a glimpse of the sorrows of Paul. This helps to ground this epistle of joy, in which Paul continually commands all Christians to "rejoice in the Lord always" (Phil 4:4).

First, let's meet Epaphroditus. As their messenger, he was entrusted with the task of bringing the money the Philippians sent to care for Paul's needs (4:18). Paul says Epaphroditus risked his life to do this (2:30). How? Paul was in prison, and his ongoing needs for food, blankets, or other necessities had to be met by a support system from outside the prison. Anyone who came to support the prisoner would be suspected too—guilt by association.

Furthermore, carrying the money from Philippi to Rome (where Paul was) would have been incredibly dangerous. Back in those days, there were no banks and no electronic wiring of funds from one account to another. Neither was there paper money. Financial support consisted entirely of gold and silver coins. These coins were heavy, and they would jingle as they were moved. So Epaphroditus risked being attacked by highway robbers. Finally, Paul says Epaphroditus became ill and almost died (2:27). Staying home, safe and sound, would have been easier for this man, but he was willing to risk his life for Paul and for the gospel.

Now let us examine Paul's sorrow. Paul says God spared Epaphroditus's life, healing him of his sickness. Though Paul supernaturally healed many people in his ministry by the power of signs and wonders (Rom 15:19), healing was by no means guaranteed (see 2 Tim 4:20). Paul undoubtedly laid hands on Epaphroditus and prayed for his healing, but he knew it would only be by the mercy of God that this faithful servant didn't die.

When at last Epaphroditus's illness broke, Paul could scarcely contain his joy. He said if God had not had mercy on this man, it would have crushed him with "sorrow upon sorrow" (2:27). This gives us a vital insight into the fact that Paul's life was essentially filled with sorrows. These sorrows included his continual persecution by the enemies of the gospel, his imprisonments and the deprivations they brought him, his physical miseries, and worst of all, the apostasy of key people who abandoned the faith at some point (e.g., Demas in 2 Tim 4:10). When we study Paul's repeated words about joy in Philippians (e.g., 3:1 and 4:4), we need to balance it with the genuine sorrows that the gospel ministry brought into Paul's life.

Perhaps the best word on this is from Paul himself, who said he was "sorrowful, yet always rejoicing" (2 Cor 6:10). I like to add one word to help me understand: "I am *sometimes* sorrowful, but always rejoicing." Or better, "My sorrows are many but fleeting, my joys are greater and eternal."

REFLECT ON CHRIST

Paul said, "For as we share abundantly in Christ's sufferings, so through Christ we share abundantly in comfort too" (2 Cor 1:5). If Epaphroditus had remained an unbeliever, he would not have been pressed into the dangers of bringing a bag of gold and silver coins to some prisoner in Rome. He would not have had to enter a Roman prison or be subjected to the filth and miseries of such a foul place. Paul himself would have continued to grow in Judaism, becoming more and more powerful and wealthier through his connections with Jewish leaders. But Christ changed everything for both of these men. They were more than willing to drink in some of the drops of sorrow that flowed out of Christ's cup, for Isaiah tells us Christ too was a "man of sorrows" (Isa 53:3). Paul says that our sufferings in this world are "light and momentary" compared to the surpassing weight of glory waiting for us in heaven (2 Cor 4:17). The consolations of Christ more than made up for their sorrows. Both

Epaphroditus and Paul were more than willing to experience the sorrows of Christ to ensure the salvation of others.

APPLY GOD'S WORD

This passage gives us a wise balance to the command "Rejoice in the Lord always" (4:4). The more we step out in faith to serve Christ, the harder our lives will get. There will be more risk, more danger, more loss. We know by faith that all of this will be eternally rewarded in heaven, but it's still hard to overcome our devotion to self-preservation. Ask God to work a spirit of faith-filled risk in you. Ask him to give you a ministry for which you are willing to suffer loss. Ask him to make you yearn for an uncommon life, a life of suffering for the gospel and for the glory of God.

PRAY

God, thank you for this teaching. Help me to set aside complacency and self-preservation to find ways to serve you that are risky. Make me aware that the more faithful I am in service to you and your gospel, the more I will share in your sorrows. Make me willing, by your Spirit. Amen.

STUDY IT FURTHER

1. Read Paul's list of sufferings again in 2 Corinthians 11:23–28. How does this help us understand Paul's statement "sorrow upon sorrow"?

2. What are you most afraid of when it comes to serving Christ wholeheartedly, especially in evangelism and missions and outreach to the poor and suffering? How could this passage help you overcome those fears?

3. Read Matthew 20:22. There Jesus asked James and John, who were looking for the honor of sitting at his right and left in his kingdom, "Are you able to drink the cup that I am to drink?" What cup is that? How is sharing in Christ's suffering related to places of honor in heaven?

Day 20

Philippians 2:29–30

READ

So receive him [Epaphroditus] in the Lord with all joy, and honor such men, for he nearly died for the work of Christ, risking his life to complete what was lacking in your service to me.

MEDITATE

In our last study, we had the chance to meet this unsung hero in the work of the Lord, Epaphroditus, and we learned about his selfless and courageous service to Paul and to the Lord. He was the messenger sent by the church at Philippi, carrying the precious gold and silver coins that the church had so lovingly collected to meet Paul's physical needs while he was in prison. The money had to be carried all the way from Philippi to Rome, possibly by boat, perhaps by caravan. In any case, Epaphroditus risked his life to make sure that the money got to Paul so that his needs would be met. He braved the dangers of highway robbers as well as other aspects of travel in the first century. And when he got there, it seems he contracted an illness serious enough that Paul thought it was likely he would die.

But Epaphroditus was so selfless that all he cared about was not being a burden for Paul or anyone else in his illness. Verse 26 tells us he was distressed because the Philippians had heard he was ill. This fits in with his entire approach to his Christian life. He did not seek a comfortable, safe life. He was willing to risk everything for the cause of the gospel, not looking for any earthly reward or praise.

Yet Paul praises him here in the text, and he strongly urges the church at Philippi to do the same. First, he wants them to receive Epaphroditus back into their midst with all joy. (Don't just merely grunt a greeting at him when he returns but celebrate his safe arrival.) Beyond that, he wants them to hold him in esteem for his willingness to suffer and even to die for the work of Christ. What does it mean to hold a man in esteem? It is a form of honor, of thinking highly of someone, of speaking words of praise and honor of him both in his presence and behind his back.

We may think this esteeming, this honoring of a human servant, is unseemly. After all, we are merely sinners saved by grace. Jesus himself abruptly cut off any seeking such honors as a motive for our service to God in Luke 17:7–10. There he speaks of a servant who serves his master without being thanked or praised. He said that we also, when we have done everything we were commanded to do, should say, "We are unworthy servants; we have only done what was our duty." While we should not seek such thanks and praise ourselves, Paul is saying we should honor people like Epaphroditus who risked his life for the gospel. At a lesser level, a healthy church should be filled with people who serve selflessly, expecting nothing, yet are consistently noticed and encouraged and honored for their service.

REFLECT ON CHRIST

When we get to heaven, this principle will be extended to our infinite time with the Father. Jesus said, "If anyone serves me, the Father will honor him" (John 12:26). That's astonishing. We are truly "unworthy servants" who have (at best) done some of our duty. None of us is perfect in our service to Christ. But as Christians, the Spirit leads us to follow Christ in service to God. If we do, God will honor us eternally for whatever we did. The greater the sacrifice, the greater the reward. God's praise for us will sound like this: "Well done, good and faithful servant. You have been faithful over a little; I will set you over much. Enter into the joy of your master" (Matt 25:23). That honor from God will not be for a moment but will last for all eternity. Christ alone will be worshiped, but all his faithful servants will be honored.

We should note that Christ acknowledges even the most seemingly insignificant acts of service by the most obscure of his servants. Remember that he singled out the widow who put two small copper coins into the offering, saying she put in more than all the others (Mark 12:44). Epaphroditus was not a famous man, not a great leader—he was nothing special. But the Holy Spirit saw fit, through Paul's words here, to honor him for twenty centuries of church history. Many such men and women, servants of Christ whose names never made it into any book, will be honored for all eternity.

APPLY GOD'S WORD

Two applications: first, find servants of Christ who are serving faithfully in some capacity and encourage them in their work. This is the simplest application of this passage. Make certain that your church is the kind of church that notes and celebrates the humble service of its members. Second, store up as much treasure in heaven as you possibly can—the treasure of praise from God (1 Cor 4:5)—by risking much for the kingdom of Christ.

PRAY

Gracious God, you are so wise in balancing this theme of honor for service rendered to Christ. On the one hand, you humble us and teach us to say, "I have only done my duty." On the other hand, you teach us to seek honor in heaven and to make sure we honor and esteem others for their service. Help us to do all of these things for the health of your church and for our own eternal joy in heaven. Amen.

STUDY IT FURTHER

1. Read Luke 17:7–10. What is Christ's purpose in telling this parable? How does this parable make you feel? How does it humble you?

2. Read John 15:5 and John 3:21. What do these passages teach us about our good works?

3. How will we be both astonishingly and radiantly honored by God in heaven and perfectly humble about all of our achievements? How can meditating on this theme help us serve Christ well now? Find someone in your church who is serving humbly and encourage him/her.

Day 21

Philippians 3:1–3

READ

Finally, my brothers, rejoice in the Lord. To write the same things to you is no trouble to me and is safe for you. Look out for the dogs, look out for the evildoers, look out for those who mutilate the flesh. For we are the circumcision, who worship by the Spirit of God and glory in Christ Jesus and put no confidence in the flesh ...

MEDITATE

Paul was constantly concerned for the health and fruitfulness of the churches he planted. He knew better than any of us the intensity of Satan's spiritual warfare against any true church of Jesus Christ. Over the last twenty centuries, Satan has consistently used three attacks to devastate local churches. Two of them are mutually exclusive: worldliness and persecution. In worldliness, Satan offers Christians the world's allurements—power, pleasures, possessions, praise. Satan did that to Jesus when he offered him the world if he would bow down and worship him (Matt 4:8–9). But if that doesn't work, Satan changes tactics and the world begins to smash Christians who will not be bought by the world's baubles. That is persecution. These two don't usually happen at the same time.

However, the third and most dangerous Satanic attack on a healthy church is false doctrine. It is the most dangerous because it has the power to pervert the teaching of the gospel itself, to entice people to follow a different gospel, which is no gospel at all (Gal 1:6–7). Paul wrote those words in Galatians because of a deadly threat to the gospel from some people called the Judaizers or the "circumcision group." They taught that faith in Christ was not enough for salvation; gentiles had to become Jews, including literal circumcision for the men and full obedience to every aspect of the law of Moses (Acts 15:5). Paul is warning the Philippians against this kind of attack—the false gospel of a combination of faith in Christ and obedience to the law of Moses. Paul calls these false teachers "dogs" and says they are evildoers who are "mutilators of the flesh" (referring to circumcision). He tells the Philippians to look out for them. Their message seems so alluring because deep inside our pride really does want to take an active role in earning our salvation.

Then Paul gives the best single-verse definition of a Christian found in the Bible: *we* are the real circumcision, we who "worship by the Spirit of God and glory in Christ Jesus and put no confidence in the flesh." First, genuine Christians are the real circumcision, an internal cutting away by the Spirit of our dead heart of rebellion against God (Rom 2:29). Second, genuine Christians worship God in the power of the Spirit. We are indwelt by the Spirit, and he moves us constantly to render praise and worship to God. Third, we rejoice (boast, glory) in Christ Jesus. The ESV has "glory," but the Greek word here really means "boast," as in a form of exultation in worship; we truly worship Jesus Christ as the Lord God in a human body. We put all our trust in him, as it is written, "Let the one who boasts, boast in the Lord" (1 Cor 1:31). This means we will spend eternity in heaven giving Jesus Christ the ultimate credit for saving our souls. Finally, we put no confidence in the flesh. That means we do not trust our own achievements, our works of obedience to the law, or any accomplishments we do in the body. Our works cannot save us, and we know it.

REFLECT ON CHRIST

I want to zero in on the statement that we glory or boast in Christ Jesus. We speak his praises now and for all eternity because we know he is worthy of them. When someone boasts pridefully in something they possess or have achieved, it is a form of self-worship. Therefore, in Jeremiah 9:23 the Lord says, "Let not the wise man boast in his wisdom, let not the mighty man boast in his might, let not the rich man boast in his riches." These are the attributes that mean the most to these people, and they are a form of idolatry. But in heaven, all the redeemed will fall before the throne of Christ and cast before him all the crowns of our honor. We will boast in the Lord openly and freely. We will be learning forever the magnitude of Christ's greatness, of what he achieved at the cross and the empty tomb, and of what the Spirit of Christ has achieved in his name since then. We will boast again and again of the greatness of Jesus Christ, and how sweet will be that eternal celebration.

APPLY GOD'S WORD

Paul began this chapter with the command, "Rejoice in the Lord" (3:1). We will have the opportunity to unfold this command when we get to chapter 4, but it is worthwhile to state it here. Everything Christ has done is for our eternal joy in him. Joy in the Lord is a good barometer of our spiritual health. We need to be aware of the three attacks on churches that I mentioned: worldliness, persecution, and false doctrine. Here Paul mentions the third, but we can apply the words "look out" to all three threats.

Unfold the statements of the single-verse definition of a Christian for yourself. As a Christian, you have been circumcised in your heart by the internal working of the Holy Spirit. God has removed from you a heart of stone and put within you a living heart (Ezek 36:26). That means that you have been made new in the core of your being. Next, realize that true Christians have the power to worship God by the Holy Spirit. Ask the Spirit to move in you, making you more passionate and powerful in worship. Next, glory in Christ Jesus as never before. Boast in him and speak of his mighty deeds. Do this in evangelism with lost people. Let them hear about Christ's greatness from you. Finally, put no confidence in the flesh whatsoever. Apart from the grace of God in Christ, you are a sinner through and through. Humble yourself before him daily.

PRAY

Father, by the Spirit we worship you, we glory in Christ,
and see our flesh's deadly weakness. Keep refining us,
that we may finish our journey of salvation. Amen.

STUDY IT FURTHER

1. Read Revelation 4:9–11. How does this passage give us a powerful sense of what true worship is and what it means to put no confidence in the flesh?

2. Read Revelation 5:1–14. How does this passage teach us what it means to glory in Christ Jesus? How could these two chapters from Revelation continually feed the healthy worship life Paul described in Philippians 3:3?

3. Why is false doctrine such a deadly attack on every local church in every generation? What are some of the most poisonous attacks on healthy doctrine you can see assaulting the church today?

Day 22

Philippians 3:4–7

READ

... though I myself have reason for confidence in the flesh also. If anyone else thinks he has reason for confidence in the flesh, I have more: circumcised on the eighth day, of the people of Israel, of the tribe of Benjamin, a Hebrew of Hebrews; as to the law, a Pharisee; as to zeal, a persecutor of the church; as to righteousness under the law, blameless. But whatever gain I had, I counted as loss for the sake of Christ.

MEDITATE

I wonder what judgment day will be like, when hundreds of millions, even billions of people will boast before the Lord of their impressive résumés of spiritual credentials. In life, they were confident of their basic goodness, the essential rightness of their claim to heaven. I meet people like this all the time in the context of evangelism. I cannot begin to guess how many people have told me in one manner or another, "I am basically a good person." These "good persons" tell me that they expect God will see that their good deeds have essentially outweighed whatever bad things they did. What a shock they are in for on that dreadful day.

Saul of Tarsus—the man we know as the apostle Paul—had a spiritual résumé of his own, and he was quite proud of it. He lists some aspects of it here, his grounds for "confidence in the flesh": first, he was circumcised "on the eighth day, of the people of Israel, of the tribe of Benjamin, a Hebrew of Hebrews" (in other words, a Jewish man, a descendant of Abraham); second, as a Pharisee, he was rigorous in his observance of the Mosaic law—this put him in a class of the spiritually elite; third, as for zeal, he was persecuting the church, hunting down Christians in his spare time, fired up by a burning passion for Israel and for the glory of God (so he supposed); and finally, concerning the law overall—blameless. Before his conversion, Paul truly believed he was blameless and had no need whatsoever for a savior. According to Paul, his spiritual résumé would have been better than anyone else's. Anyone who was not a Jew would have been ruled out immediately as a pagan idolater, following the false gods of the nations. Moreover, any other Jew was far behind him because he was "advancing in Judaism" beyond his contemporaries through his relentless zeal for the Mosaic law (Gal 1:14).

But Paul came to realize all such spiritual credentials are "loss" rather than "gain" (v. 7), even "rubbish" (v. 8). Spiritual pride is a stench in the nostrils of God, for it ultimately denies any need for a savior. As Paul says in Galatians 2:21, "If righteousness were through the law [i.e., by human achievement], then Christ died for no purpose." Almighty God burns with an infinite zeal for the glory of his Son and for his death on the cross. There can be no salvation apart from Christ's cross, and our boasting in our spiritual credentials is obnoxious to the Lord. He will not spend eternity with people who boast in themselves. Therefore, every aspect of God's saving work in us is designed by his wisdom to humble us.

REFLECT ON CHRIST

This deep humbling work of the Spirit in the gospel is essential to our salvation. It contains the sting of conviction that we are sinners who cannot save ourselves, but it also has the infinitely delightful realization of the perfect righteousness of Christ as our hope. To receive this perfect righteousness as a gift, freely, by faith alone, is truly humbling. It will be the focus of our eternal praise of Jesus in heaven. Christ's résumé is staggering. His deity is established in the assertion Paul gave in Philippians 2:6, that Christ was in the form of God. His human lineage as the son of David and the son of Abraham (Matt 1:1) is perfect. His entire life was lived perfectly in obedience to the law of Moses and the meticulous will of his Father, for he stated, "I always do the things that are pleasing to him" (John 8:29). Every word he ever spoke was exactly what his Father told him to say (John 8:28). His mighty works of healing were done in fulfillment of the commandment to love your neighbor as yourself. His death on the cross was in perfect obedience to the command of his Father. He has the only perfect résumé that there has ever been, and it is ours by simple faith in Christ.

APPLY GOD'S WORD

We all have that tendency inside us to boast of our works or to flaunt our spiritual credentials. It is a deep-seated, stubborn tendency in us all. We need to ask God to eradicate that boasting forever. It has already been said of us that we boast "in Christ Jesus and put no confidence in the flesh" (3:3). Let that be increasingly true of you. Let Paul's final appraisal of his spiritual résumé humble you and cause you to turn away from your own forever. Ask the Lord to show you times that you boast of your service or your spiritual attributes. Ask him to humble you and show you that these things are loss and rubbish if you seek to present them as the basis of your relationship with God. More and more, speak words of humility about yourself and words of exaltation concerning Christ.

PRAY

Gracious and patient God, I know that spiritual pride is repugnant to you. Please root it out of me. Make me truly aware that I am nothing apart from the gift of Christ's perfect righteousness. Amen.

STUDY IT FURTHER

1. Picture in your mind the redeemed from every nation on earth (Rev 7:9). Identify what you are tempted to be most proud of in your spiritual life—an achievement, habit, character trait, or talent. Then imagine how many of your brothers and sisters in Christ from all over the world and from every century of church history might have similar attributes in their Christian lives. Where do you think you would rank among the hundreds of thousands who shared those same traits? Does this humble you?

2. Again, look at those traits of yours, your résumé. Go through each aspect and humble yourself before God about each one. Tell God, "My best attributes are not good enough for heaven even as

the best garment of a field peasant would not have been good enough for the palace." Then tell God, "All of my good traits are given by you, purchased by the blood of Christ, worked in me by the Spirit."

3. Finally, meditate on the perfect righteousness of Christ: his achievements, attributes, and character. See the beauty of each one and thank God that all of it has been credited to your account. Let that bring you peace and joy today.

Day 23

Philippians 3:8–9

READ

Indeed, I count everything as loss because of the surpassing worth of knowing Christ Jesus my Lord. For his sake I have suffered the loss of all things and count them as rubbish, in order that I may gain Christ and be found in him, not having a righteousness of my own that comes from the law, but that which comes through faith in Christ, the righteousness from God that depends on faith ...

MEDITATE AND REFLECT ON CHRIST

These may be some of the most passionate words of worship ever written for the Lord Jesus Christ. The apostle Paul, moved by the Holy Spirit, perhaps even weeping as he wrote them, poured out the deepest love of his heart. It is an eternal love worked in him by the Holy Spirit, and it began the moment he saw Christ in resurrected glory on the road to Damascus. Paul gives a sense of his appraisal of the worth and value of Christ. He speaks of "counting" things loss and rubbish compared to the surpassing excellence of knowing Christ Jesus our

Lord. Everything in the world has value when appraised. An art appraiser can give the market value of an antique oil painting; a jeweler can look at the facets of a diamond—its cut and clarity and weight—and give an appraisal of its value. Paul has looked at everything in his life (indeed in the whole universe) and considers it loss and rubbish compared to the excellence of the knowledge of Christ. Nothing is worth more than that to Paul.

This rare jewel, like the treasure hidden in the field or the pearl of great value, caused Paul to gladly give up everything he had that he might obtain it. He burned all the bridges with the Pharisees and the Sanhedrin that he might pursue knowing Christ. It was worth it to him. On the road to Damascus, he caught the briefest glimpse of the glory of Christ, and it made him endlessly thirsty for more—more and more knowledge of Christ. This rare jewel of knowing Christ came in five facets for Paul. We'll walk through each of these over three studies. The first two facets are:

1. *Personal knowledge of Christ:* This is factual as well as personal, relational knowledge of him. Paul would never stop yearning to know everything he could about Jesus Christ, "in whom are hidden all the treasures of wisdom and knowledge" (Col 2:3). Paul could say to Jesus:

    - I want to know what you taught, all your words; I want to memorize your teachings line by line.
    - I want to know the story of your life—every event, every temptation you resisted, every conflict with the Scribes and Pharisees, every interaction with a humble sinner seeking healing.

- I want to know all of your miracles, how they demonstrated your character, your love, your compassion, your power over demons.
- I want to know how you considered it joy to die on the cross for my sins.
- I want to know why you wept over Jerusalem and at Lazarus's tomb.
- I want to know why you sweated great drops of blood when you prayed in Gethsemane.
- I want to know your humility, your love, your gentleness, your tenderness for your sheep.
- I want to understand how God the Father created all things through you.
- I want to know how you uphold and sustain all things by the word of your power.

Paul had tasted the goodness and power of Christ; he had seen some of his resurrection glory; he had tasted the power and glory of the coming age, and he deeply wanted more. That one vision of Christ transformed everything for Paul. He would never be the same again, nor would his tastes, his desires, or his yearnings. Paul could say, "I have tasted Christ, but I want more. I have known Christ, but I want to know him more."

The infinite person of Christ draws forth from the redeemed an infinite thirst for knowledge of him. A large part of eternity in heaven is for this education. It has begun here on earth, but it will fill all eternity.

2. *The gift of righteousness through faith in Christ*: Paul wanted to be found "in him, not having a righteousness of my own that comes from the law, but that which comes through faith in Christ, the righteousness from God that depends on faith" (Phil 3:9). Paul had rejected his own righteousness as rubbish. To know Christ is to be clothed with Christ, to be "found in him." The "finding" is by God himself, the judge of all the earth, who sees all Christians in Christ positionally, clothed in Christ's righteousness, which alone is sufficient for heaven. Paul treasured that righteousness and stood in it blameless. He stands in it still.

APPLY GOD'S WORD

Paul's incessant yearning to know Christ should kindle inside each one of us a similar holy passion. We should be done with lesser things, the worldly things that titillate our senses but do not satisfy our souls. We should pursue knowing Christ, and as part of that pursuit, develop an increasing, escalating, accelerating longing to know him more and more. If we do not feel this burning desire, it is clear evidence of the hardening effects of sin in its deceitfulness (Heb 3:12–13). Ask God to give you this ardent passion, this deep thirst for Christ. Ask the Spirit to reveal Christ to you and give you enough to go on, so that you will soon come back for more. The apostle Paul knew Christ better in this world than anyone else in church history, and he still yearned to know him better. What about us? Ask the Spirit to drive out idols that are blunting your desire for Christ. Ask the Spirit to show you worldly habits that are filling your mind and heart with rubbish when you could be feasting on Christ. It is the Spirit's unique role in our lives to reveal Christ inside us. Ask God to pour out fresh effusions of the Spirit to this end of knowing Christ more and more.

PRAY

Lord, we yearn to know you more and more. We know that you are the true treasure hidden in the field. Help us to be willing to sell everything, whatever that means, so that we may open the treasure box and begin taking out its jewels one by one. Amen.

STUDY IT FURTHER

1. In Revelation 5:1–3, a search is made in heaven and on earth and under the earth for someone who is worthy to take a scroll from God's hand and open it. No one was found worthy—not a single created being in the universe. The apostle John wept because of this. But an angel told him not to weep, for the Lion of the Tribe of Judah—Jesus Christ—is worthy. However, this Lion looked like a Lamb that had been slain (Rev 5:6). How does this vision line up with the passage we are studying in Philippians 3? How does it show the amazing attributes of Christ?

2. To support this idea further, look up Jonathan Edwards's great sermon on Revelation 5 entitled "The Excellency of Christ." Read it and allow it to move you to worship Christ for his surpassing greatness.

Day 24

Philippians 3:10

READ

... that I may know him and the power of his resurrection, and may share his sufferings, becoming like him in his death ...

MEDITATE AND REFLECT ON CHRIST

In the last study, we began walking through this magnificent passage from Paul, a passage which expresses the greatest joy and deepest longing of his heart in one phrase: knowing Christ. We saw that these words show knowing Christ is like a diamond with five sparkling facets. Last time we covered: (1) knowledge of Christ, both factual and relational; and (2) the gift of righteousness through faith in Christ. These two facets were so glorious for Paul that he was willing to count all things a loss that he might "gain Christ and be found in him." To "gain Christ" clearly implies that the great apostle Paul felt he had yet to acquire all of Christ that he could, and there was infinitely more yet to come. He says in verse 10 "that I may know him." There will be no end to this education, this expedition of discovery.

Then he says he wants to become "like him in his death" that Christ's righteousness would be credited to him by faith. Let's look at two more radiant facets from these verses:

1. *The power of Christ's resurrected life inside him:* Paul wants to know the spiritual power of Christ's resurrection in his soul. (Paul will also speak of his own bodily resurrection; that will be facet five, which we will discuss in the next study.) The power of Christ's resurrection is limitless, destroying all invisible chains and barriers that Satan and sin and death wrap around our souls. In Romans 6:1–14, Paul speaks of our spiritual union with Christ in his death and his resurrection. By that union we have died to sin and live to God. By that union we can walk in newness of life, free from the power of sin every single moment. To know the power of Christ's resurrection right now in our souls means to put every temptation to death and to surge with spiritual energy in a river of good works. This resurrection power is available to us every moment of our earthly lives by Christ's Spirit who lives within us. Paul says he wants to know that power more and more.

2. *The fellowship of Christ's sufferings, being conformed to his death:* Paul amazingly yearns to know Christ in his suffering. He had perhaps suffered more than any Christian of his day or since. Yet rather than seeking to avoid more pain, he embraced it as the best way to draw close in spiritual intimacy with Christ. There is a sweet fellowship in sharing in Christ's sufferings because he pours out his

Spirit in fresh waves on all who suffer for his name (1 Pet 4:13–14). It would not surprise me at all to find out that when Paul and Silas were singing in the dark Philippian jail with their backs bleeding and their feet fastened in the stocks, the Lord poured into them a supernatural joy and peace, a foretaste of heaven on earth that is impossible to put into words. Paul writes of a "peace which surpasses all understanding" that guards our hearts and minds in Christ Jesus (Phil 4:7). Paul had experienced that many times in his sorrows. In Corinth, the Lord encouraged Paul in a vision (Acts 18:9). Later, in a severe storm, the Lord sent an angel to tell him he would survive the shipwreck (Acts 27:23). When he was all alone on trial for his life before Caesar, the Lord himself stood at Paul's side and gave him strength (2 Tim 4:17). Paul was willing to stand with Jesus in his rejection and humiliation "outside the camp, bearing his reproach" (Heb 13:13) because he knew it would result in a tremendous sense of closeness with Jesus. Nothing was more important than that. Beyond that, however, Paul knew that only by suffering can we be perfectly conformed to Christ in his death. It is by dying to self that we rise again spiritually to new life. Nothing is harder for us than this, taking up our cross and following Jesus to death.

APPLY GOD'S WORD

These verses call us to move out and follow Jesus Christ wherever he may lead us. They promise a level of intimacy with Christ that we can hardly imagine and give us a foretaste of the very essence of the heavenly life, which is knowing God and Jesus Christ fully (John 17:3). To feel the surge of Christ's resurrection power in our souls as we boldly minister for him is a treasure beyond all words. It drives away the deadness and lethargy of a worldly life lived for selfish desires. The level beyond that is a willingness to know Christ in his sufferings—the rejection and abuse he suffered from sinners, his painful and shameful death on the cross. Jesus asked James and John, "Are you able to drink the cup I drink?" (Mark 10:38). That is the fellowship of sharing in his sufferings, with the goal being conformity to Christ in his death. These verses call us to follow Christ and become like him in ways we have never dreamed of before. Today, if you hear his voice, do not harden your hearts, but follow him.

PRAY

Our Lord, you are the glory that will illuminate the New Jerusalem for all eternity, and you graciously allow us to have that light glowing in our souls right now. Grant me a willingness to suffer the pain of dying to myself. Give me the strength to follow you, Lord! Amen.

STUDY IT FURTHER

1. Amy Carmichael was not a martyr (meaning she was not executed for her faith in Christ), but she spoke of difficult service to Christ as "a chance to die." Track down that quote and read it in context. Ask the Lord to show you how you could find "a chance to die" for Christ in your life.

2. Get a copy of *Foxe's Book of Martyrs* by John Foxe. Read a few martyr stories to your family or to some friends. Ask the Lord to open your eyes to the courage these martyrs

had for Christ. Especially study how their sufferings opened up intimacy with Christ.

3. What do you fear most when it comes to suffering for Christ? Write down your fears and ask the Lord to help you conquer them by faith.

Day 25

Philippians 3:11

READ

... that by any means possible I may attain the resurrection from the dead.

MEDITATE AND REFLECT ON CHRIST

For a third time, we are meditating on Paul's yearning to know Christ, a knowledge Paul considered more precious than anything else in the universe. We have seen four of the five facets of this glittering diamond: (1) personal knowledge of Christ, both factual and relational; (2) the gift of Christ's righteousness through faith; (3) the spiritual power of Christ's resurrection at work in his life; (4) the fellowship of Christ's sufferings resulting in conformity to Christ's death. Now we will meditate on the final and most glorious goal of Paul's life: his own bodily resurrection from the dead. Paul's assertion is that all of these aspects of knowing Christ will culminate in his glorious resurrection from the dead—they all serve that end. It is only by knowing facts about Christ that faith in him can form, and those facts come as a living reality: Christ is alive and wants a relationship with Paul. This knowledge leads to faith, and faith in Christ justifies a sinner like Paul, providing full forgiveness of all sins and a righteous standing in Christ. Faith in Christ is the first spiritual action of a new life in Christ that comes by our spiritual union with him, being "found in him." Then this new life in Christ expands into ever-increasing knowledge of him day after day. It is amazing that the man who wrote the book of Romans, who was caught up into the third heaven and saw the heavenly glory of the Son of God, knew that his knowledge of Christ was still a tiny fraction of what it could be and would be. Despite all his great knowledge of Christ in every respect, he still yearned—burned—for more. This daily pursuit of knowing Christ led him (as we saw in our last study) to be willing to join him in his sufferings. Only by this participation in Christ would he be conformed to Christ in his death.

This kind of life is the only one that leads to the ultimate end of Christ's saving mission—the resurrection of his beloved people from the dead. What is the point of knowing Christ for the brief time in this world if it all ends in death? If there is no resurrection from the dead, then as Ecclesiastes 9:5 says, "The dead know nothing." But Christ gave this glorious definition of our ultimate salvation in his prayer to God: "And this is eternal life, that they may know you, the only true God, and Jesus Christ whom you have sent" (John 17:3). Our eternal life, which begins at the moment of saving faith, makes progress in this world by knowing Christ more and more and will extend into eternity by an unending education in the glory of God and of Christ in heaven. Thus, all four aspects of knowing Christ that Paul yearns for in Philippians 3:7–11 lead to resurrection from the dead and the beginning of the perfected life of heaven. But the quest for knowing Christ will never end. Why? Because we will never be omniscient, not even in heaven, and Christ will never run out of aspects of his glory to reveal to us.

When Paul concludes this display of his deepest yearning (to know Christ) with the words "if by any means I may attain to the resurrection from the dead," he echoes the deepest yearning of Christ's own heart for him. For in that same prayer mentioned above, Jesus prays, "Father, I desire that they also, whom you have given me, may be with me where I am, to see my glory that you have given me because you loved me before the foundation of the world" (John 17:24). Jesus wants Paul (and all the elect) to know him; Paul (and all the elect) deeply yearns to know him. This yearning is the basis of the mysterious and eternal "marriage" of the bridegroom (Christ) and the bride (the church) that will be consummated in heaven.

APPLY GOD'S WORD

To apply this passage fully and powerfully, we should seek Christ by the Spirit more than ever before. We should set our hearts fully and daily on things above and things to come (Col 3:1–2). We should make knowing more about Christ factually, experiencing Christ more spiritually, and suffering with Christ more willingly the top priorities of our daily lives. We should realize that our time here on earth is brief, that death is inevitable, that heaven is "better by far," and that knowing Christ is the purpose of every one of the finite number of days we have left here on earth.

Today, as you finish this devotional, ask Jesus to reveal himself to you in a fresh way. Ask him to make you willing to serve him today. Ask him to prepare you to suffer and to die to yourself today. Nothing is harder, for our flesh claws and clamors and resists this journey of knowing Christ every moment of every day. Expect the Spirit to show you Christ in both the mundane and the extraordinary moments of life. And prepare to grow in ways you've ever experienced in your Christian life.

PRAY

Lord, every day is a preparation for the true life that will begin after my resurrection from the dead. Help me to set my heart fully on that grace that you will give me at that moment. Amen.

STUDY IT FURTHER

1. Read again the description of the resurrection body in 1 Corinthians 15:42–44. Study how Paul describes it, the words he uses. Allow your heart to be filled with joy at the future resurrection body. We will study this again later in this devotional.

2. Read John 6:37–44. Count the number of times Jesus promises to raise up his people on the last day. How do his words fill you with hope?

3. As you ponder your resurrection from the dead, how can it free you from fear of disease, injury, and aging? What aspects of these three things—disease, injury, and aging—cause you the most anxiety? How could Philippians 3:7–11 help you overcome that anxiety?

Day 26

Philippians 3:12–14

READ

Not that I have already obtained it or have already become perfect, but I press on so that I may lay hold of that for which also I was laid hold of by Christ Jesus. Brethren, I do not regard myself as having laid hold of it yet; but one thing I do: forgetting what lies behind and reaching forward to what lies ahead, I press on toward the goal for the prize of the upward call of God in Christ Jesus. (NASB)

MEDITATE

Perfection—that is the goal of my Christian life. Absolute, total perfection. Amazingly, that quest should be the goal of every Christian on earth. Usually, when we speak of someone on a quest for perfection, we may think of an imbalanced person, an extremist with no sense of the reality of the world we're living in. We may know some examples of people who pursue perfection in some detail of life like a sculptor, seeking to perfect his craft in a single sculpture; or a violinist, seeking the perfect rendition of a Bach concerto; or a gymnast, seeking the perfect routine on the balance beam. We may admire their dedication and acknowledge that such a quest does have merits, but it is extremely rarely attained. Moreover, that solitary quest for perfection in one narrow aspect of life inevitably has consequences in other areas of a person's life—no social life, rudeness and irritability toward anyone who gets in their way, arrogance, and more. Yet Paul is not looking for perfection in one area of life, but in *all* areas of life—absolute, total conformity to Christ in every possible way. Perfect in mind, in heart, in will, in affection, in emotion, even in body. Perfect love for God; perfect love for others. A perfect thought life. Perfect motives for every action. Perfect in prayer. Perfect in every temptation. Perfect purity—absolute freedom from every evil. Pure light, as God himself is pure light.

Paul acknowledges that he has not attained this yet, but every single day he *presses on* toward that goal. The Holy Spirit within him never tells him it is acceptable to sin in this way, as long as you don't sin in that way. No! All sin is evil; all sin is poison. Paul wants to be perfectly conformed to Christ in holiness. This "pressing on" displays the intense effort the Christian life requires. It is warfare; it is not effortless ease. It is not "let go and let God." It is putting sin to death by the Spirit (Rom 8:13). To attain this goal is the intense focus of Paul's life. He says it is the "one thing I do." To attain this goal requires his total concentration, forgetting what was behind him (both his victories and his defeats), pressing on after the "upward call of God in Christ Jesus." He turns his face upward, always higher in Christ. Relentless.

There are three amazing things about this quest for Christian perfection: first, it is commanded by God, for Christ said, "You therefore must be perfect, as your heavenly Father is perfect" (Matt 5:48); second, it can never be attained in this life, as Paul says twice in this passage; third, it is guaranteed. Paul says it is the very purpose for which Christ laid hold of him (v. 12). Christ will never let Paul go. He will finish the purpose—the perfection—for which he laid hold of him.

REFLECT ON CHRIST

This perfection is total conformity to Christ. That is God's eternal purpose in predestination, according to Romans 8:29. God wants all of the elect to spend all of eternity totally conformed to Christ. Our bodies will be conformed to Christ's glorious, resurrection body (Phil 3:21). Our minds will be conformed to Christ's mind, so that we will only think of things that are true, noble, just, pure, lovely, of good report, virtuous, and praiseworthy (Phil 4:8). Our affections will be perfectly conformed to Christ's affection, for we will love righteousness and hate wickedness like he does (Heb 1:8). And our wills will be perfectly conformed to Christ's will, for God will have worked in us both to will and to do according to his good pleasure for all eternity (Phil 2:12–13), and God's will finally will be done on earth as it is in heaven (Matt 6:10).

To realize that Christ already displayed this perfection while he lived on earth is staggering. Yet perhaps it is even more staggering that he is working in us sinners now by his Spirit to make us just as perfect as he is.

APPLY GOD'S WORD

Dear Christian reader, you should meditate deeply on this relentless quest for perfection. Understand that verse 12 tells you that Jesus took hold of you in the unbreakable grip of grace the moment you were born again into the family of God. He forgave all your sins (past, present, and future). He intends that you should not stay where you were when he took hold of you. He took hold of you for a purpose—that you should be conformed to his perfection forever and ever. Now, he commands you to do what Paul did in the grip of grace—press on, press on, press on after perfection every day. Do not slack a moment in your yearning for Christlike perfection. Wherever you see sin, crush it by the Spirit. Understand that this race for perfection will take all the energy you have every day of your life for the rest of your life. But also be filled with hope, because this upward call of God in Christ Jesus for the prize of heavenly perfection will most certainly be rewarded. When you die, or when the Lord descends from heaven at the end of the world, you will be transformed into glory in an instant by his power. Meanwhile, he exhorts us to forget what lies behand and reach forward to what lies ahead.

PRAY

O Lord, you have taken hold of me in the unbreakable grip of grace. Satan cannot break that grip, neither can the world with all of its allurements and attacks, nor my own inner corruptions. You took hold of me for a clear purpose: that I might someday be perfect, holy, and blameless in your sight. Give me a relentless drive after perfect holiness today by your Spirit. Amen.

STUDY IT FURTHER

1. Philippians 3:12 is a complex verse. Different translations render it different ways, but there is a strong sense of Christ first taking hold of you and doing so for a purpose—your eternal perfection in heaven. How does his purposeful grip on you fill you with hope as you battle sin?

2. Why do you think perfectionism is usually harmful? Why is the pursuit of perfection in this section very healthy? What's the difference between the two?

3. How do you picture perfection in heaven? How does it relate to Christlikeness? How does developing a stronger sense of heavenly Christlike perfection help us fight sin now?

Day 27

Philippians 3:15–17

READ

Let those of us who are mature think this way, and if in anything you think otherwise, God will reveal that also to you. Only let us hold true to what we have attained. Brothers, join in imitating me, and keep your eyes on those who walk according to the example you have in us.

MEDITATE

In teaching about paying taxes, Jesus asked for a denarius and showed the Pharisees and Herodians Caesar's image and inscription (Mark 12:16). The coin was minted with this image and inscription by force. The soft precious metal (silver or gold) was struck by something called the *typos* or the "pattern." The hard *typos* would cause the softer silver or gold to take on its image so that every coin looked the same. This is the word Paul uses for himself as a role model in the Christian life in today's passage (v. 17). He wants every Christian to think and live the same way he does, which is patterned after Christ.

Paul is one of the greatest Christian role models in the history of the church. In Philippians 3:7–14, he describes the "pattern" for the Christian life. It is a life completely centered on knowing Christ in all respects: knowing him factually through the word; knowing him experientially through the Spirit-filled life; knowing the power of Christ's resurrection spiritually through daily obedience; knowing Christ also in his sufferings, being conformed to him in his death; and ultimately hoping in the consummation of salvation through the bodily resurrection from the dead. The Christian life is one of relentless pursuit after Christlike perfection, knowing we'll never attain it in this life but will most certainly attain it in the next. According to Paul, this way of looking at the Christian life in this world is most certainly the right one. He says all the mature, those who have been in Christ for a while and who have made significant progress in him, should "have this mind" (i.e., this same attitude toward growing in Christ).

If there are any who disagree with this model, Paul is patient with them. He doesn't yell at them or rebuke them. He says, at some point, God will reveal the truth to them. It is as if Paul were saying, "I'm not wrong about all this. Someday you'll see it the way I do." But in the meantime, every Christian should live up to the level of Christian understanding that they have attained. That will involve some level of the same kind of lifestyle, this relentless pressing after perfection in Christ.

Paul invites all his readers (including us) to follow his example, and not just his but anyone else's who is living this kind of life in the pattern of Christ. A healthy church will be made up of many mature men and women who are able to present their godly lives as role models for younger Christians to imitate. In America, we seem to love and celebrate rugged individualism, and we honor the maverick who charts a whole new course. But Christian maturity is marked by submitting to the pattern that Paul lays out in Philippians 3:7–14. When the *typos* smashes the blank coin, it forces the softer metal to adopt its image, its perfect conformity. So we must be spiritually "soft" to take on Christ's image; we must yield and not be stubborn, hard-hearted, or stiff-necked.

REFLECT ON CHRIST

As we've been saying throughout this chapter, Jesus Christ is ultimately the pattern to which all Christians will be conformed. Paul wrote plainly in Romans 8:29 that God predestined each elect person to be "conformed to the image of his Son, in order that he might be the firstborn among many brothers." When we receive our resurrection bodies in the new heaven and new earth, we will be surrounded by an innumerable multitude of fellow Christians from every nation and language and culture on earth. All of us will have been perfectly conformed to Christ while retaining our identity as individuals. Our fellowship with our brothers and sisters will be eternally rich and diverse, but every one of us will have the mind of Christ and the heart of Christ, and we will glow with the glory of Christ.

In the meantime, we are called to submit to the conforming process of sanctification each day. Paul calls us to live up to what we have already received in Christ and then build on it day by day. What we know about Christ already is enough to cause us to fall on our faces in worship every single day for the rest of our lives, but he has so much more to teach us. Paul knew that and simply said, "I want to know Christ." This is our calling.

APPLY GOD'S WORD

This concept of the "pattern" is a powerful one. God is moving to conform us to Christ. It is not our individuality that God is celebrating but rather the degree to which we are like his Son. We need to come to him humbly in prayer and ask the Lord to conform us more and more to him, to mold us into his perfect image. We should be aware of this and yearn for it, not remaining satisfied with however much progress we have already made.

Beyond this, we should seek to become role models for others. Perhaps that is beyond you at this point—maybe you are just beginning the Christian journey. Ask God to make you a role model in the future and seek such a role model now. Imitate your mentor as that person imitates Christ.

But if you have already been mentored and are, as Paul says, "mature," then be a role model for someone else. Men with men, and women with women. Healthy churches are full of such mentors, and if it is time for you, then seek out someone and pour into that young Christian's life.

PRAY

Almighty God, from eternity past you planned that your chosen children would be perfectly conformed to your only begotten Son. I am one of those children by your grace. Keep working in me, conforming me to Christ. Do this in me today by the power of your Spirit. Then help me to mentor others in the Christian life. Amen.

STUDY IT FURTHER

1. Read 2 Timothy 2:2. How does that verse speak about four generations of Christian mentors? How is such a pattern of spiritual multiplication vital for the spread of the gospel around the world?

2. Another use of the Greek word *typos* ("pattern") is in 2 Timothy 1:13. What is the "pattern" there? How do these two patterns, godly living (Phil 3:17) and sound doctrine (2 Tim 1:13), combine in a healthy discipleship plan?

3. Why do you think people in Western cultures celebrate individualism? How is conformity to the patterns of sound doctrine and holy living superior to charting our own course in the Christian life? How does it allow for some measure of individual uniqueness?

Day 28

Philippians 3:18–19

READ

For many, of whom I have often told you and now tell you even with tears, walk as enemies of the cross of Christ. Their end is destruction, their god is their belly, and they glory in their shame, with minds set on earthly things.

MEDITATE

George Mueller, who lived in England in the nineteenth century and was one of the most compassionate and effective ministers to orphans in church history, once gave a compelling insight into the goal of his daily quiet time: "The first great and primary business to which I ought to attend every day is to have my soul happy in the Lord."[1] He argued that there was no point in him rising from his time in Scripture and prayer without reestablishing his connection with Christ, resulting in the joy of the Lord as his strength. This certainly harmonizes with the command Paul gives three times in this epistle, "Rejoice in the

1. Quoted by John Piper, *Desiring God* (Colorado Springs: Multnomah Press, 1996), 132).

Lord" (Phil 3:1; 4:4 [x2]). But there is another dimension that could just as reasonably be argued to be the goal of our quiet times. It is the very thing we have seen as the overall goal of the Christian life in Philippians 3:7–14: to know Christ and thereby to be increasingly conformed to him. This is our salvation—total conformity to Christ. Part of that conformity is not merely to rejoice in him but to *weep with him*.

Jesus Christ was a "man of sorrows and acquainted with grief" (Isa 53:3). Certainly, the ultimate goal of his life, death, and resurrection was to bring us to God, in whose presence is the "fullness of joy," at whose right hand are "pleasures forevermore" (Ps 16:11). Certainly, Christ endured the pain and the shame of the cross "for the joy that was set before him" (Heb 12:2). But in the meantime, while so many are still in bondage to sin and running on a broad road that leads to hell (Matt 7:13), Jesus showed his heart of compassion by weeping over lost Jerusalem (Luke 19:41). Our present conformity to Christ must mean the same for us. We must learn to have our hearts shredded over the plight of the perishing in this present age.

Paul certainly did. In Romans 9:2, Paul cries out that he has "great sorrow and unceasing anguish" in his heart for perishing Jews who were rejecting Christ. In today's passage, we see the same grief. Paul reminds the Philippians of what he had told them many times before: many are living every day as enemies of the cross of Christ. Their "god is their belly," meaning they live for fleshly drives like food, drink, sex, and sensual pleasures. They glory in the very things that will bring them eternal shame. If they do not repent, they will end up cast into the lake of fire, screaming in torment for all eternity. These are the very ones that are keeping Paul in chains and persecuting the church in Philippi. Paul doesn't hate them. He weeps for them with deep and bitter tears, and he yearns for the Philippians to do the same.

REFLECT ON CHRIST

Paul said he wanted to join Christ "in the fellowship of his sufferings, being conformed to his death" (Phil 3:10 NASB). Paul's tears for his enemies show how far that conformity had gone in Paul's life. Paul was flogged five times, beaten with rods three times, and stoned once (2 Cor 11:24–25). He was imprisoned again and again, sometimes left in prison for years to please his Jewish enemies (Acts 24:27). But instead of embittering Paul and filling him with a desire for revenge, this suffering molded his soul more and more into the image of his Savior, Jesus Christ. Jesus is the one who cried out concerning his murderers, "Father, forgive them, for they know not what they do" (Luke 23:34). To be able to see beyond the immediate circumstances to the spiritual reality of souls whose "end is destruction" and yearn for their forgiveness by almighty God is the most Christlike a person can become in this world.

APPLY GOD'S WORD

Do you weep for the lost? This is an extremely convicting question. I truly believe that the main reason Christians do not fervently pray for lost people and courageously witness to them is that we do not see their eternal state properly and do not sufficiently care. Simply put, we don't weep for the lost as Jesus and Paul did. Today's text calls on us to repent—not just to seek to be "happy in the Lord" but to be conformed to Christ in this matter. We may spend today surrounded by people just like the ones Paul described in this text: people who hate the cross of Christ, whose god is their stomach, whose glory is in their shame. Instead of being angry or annoyed at their sin, we need to ask God to do a deep work of compassion in us. We need to meditate on what the Bible teaches about hell—eternal conscious torment. Jesus described it as a place of utter darkness where there will be "weeping and gnashing of teeth" (Matt 8:12). We need to see the lost as if they are drowning in a lagoon and we are on the shore. Are we willing to dive in, swim out to them, take them in our arms while their blind panic causes them to thrash at us, and draw them safely to shore?

PRAY

Lord Jesus, you wept over Jerusalem. You molded your servant Paul to weep over his enemies. Forgive me for my indifference to the spiritual state and final destination of the lost in my world. Please break my heart. Teach me to weep for them as I have never wept before. Let that grief move me to sacrificial actions to reach as many as you place before me. Amen.

STUDY IT FURTHER

1. Read the account of Jesus weeping over Jerusalem (Luke 19:41–44). How does his example move you to care more about the lost? What does Jesus's extreme sorrow over lostness teach you about his heart?

2. Read Romans 9:1–3. Why is it particularly astonishing that Paul would have such a level of sorrow for the lost among the Jewish nation? What do you think of his statement that, in effect, he would be willing to trade his salvation if it could rescue them from hell?

3. What are some practical ways we can grow in compassion for lost people? How would rubbing shoulders with lost people more regularly help?

Day 29

Philippians 3:20

READ

But our citizenship is in heaven, and from it we await a Savior, the Lord Jesus Christ.

MEDITATE

During Paul's time, citizenship in the Roman Empire was extremely valuable. Sometimes Caesar would bequeath to an individual or even a city and its surrounding region the honor of Roman citizenship as a reward for sacrificial service to Rome. Sometimes non-Romans would pay exorbitant fees to become citizens of Rome, as did the tribune who tried Paul in Acts 22:28. Paul was born a citizen of Rome, and several times he used that status to rescue himself from legal danger. He stopped that tribune from beating him, a Roman citizen who hadn't been found guilty, and he was able to escape his Jewish accusers in Palestine by appealing directly to Caesar (Acts 25:11). Paul's Roman citizenship was precious to him, but his true citizenship was in heaven. The moment he was adopted as a child of God, he entered the kingdom of Christ. That made him forever a citizen of heaven. Any advantages that came to him as a Roman citizen were limited and temporal, but the advantages of being a citizen of heaven were limitless and eternal. This concept of being a citizen of heaven lines up very well with the faith of the patriarchs described in Hebrews 11:13–16. They died in faith, not receiving the promised land or any of the best promises of God. They died looking forward to a heavenly city and country that would be their eternal home, their glorious reward. They died confessing that they were aliens and strangers in this world. Because their hearts were so completely set on the heavenly city and heavenly country that they could only see by faith, God was not ashamed to be called their God. For them, and for all who die in the faith of the gospel, God is preparing a home.

Essential to this life of faith, this acknowledgment that our citizenship is in heaven, is our eager expectation of the second coming of Christ. The life of faith is forward-looking, as Paul wrote in Colossians 3:4, "When Christ who is your life appears, then you also will appear with him in glory." We'll talk more fully about that glory in our next study. For now, let us focus on the eager expectation of the coming of the Lord that characterizes all healthy Christians in this world. We truly are aliens and strangers in this present age, and we must resist the constant allure of this world and all its supposed advantages.

REFLECT ON CHRIST

In the end, Paul focused his meditation on Christ and his coming kingdom. He spoke of us all eagerly awaiting Christ's second coming and the perfect realm he would establish at that time. Then, at last, all the times God's people have begged him to make "his kingdom come" so that "his will would be done on earth as it is in heaven" will come true. Christ is our life, our glory, our future. However, many may be the advantages and delights of our present earthly citizenship, all of them are limited and temporary as were Paul's as a Roman citizen. It is right for us to be thankful and to use those advantages as Paul did for the spread of the kingdom of Christ, but we must hold all such allegiances and delights far below what we owe to Christ. The Roman tribune paid a huge sum of gold coins for his Roman citizenship. Christ paid for our heavenly citizenship with his blood.

Let that thought sink in. As needed, let it reorient your priorities and allegiances. At some point, we will be lying on our deathbeds, about to cross over into eternity. At that moment, any advantages our earthly citizenship gave us will disappear, but our heavenly citizenship will soon be consummated. We will be lifted up into a glorious world to spend eternity submitting gladly to our heavenly Lord and his perfect government. Set your mind fully on that.

APPLY GOD'S WORD

My earthly citizenship is with the United States of America. I believe that the political system of freedoms in this country established by the constitution is one of the best this world has to offer. I am aware that these freedoms were bought by the blood of soldiers and have been defended again and again. I am aware that American citizenship gives me many advantages, and for those I am grateful, but I do not idolize citizenship in this country. Like Paul, I know that my true citizenship is in heaven. There will be no patriotism in heaven, no yearning for a return to the earthly status we had in this world. We will be subjects of a new kingdom, citizens of an eternal nation. Nebuchadnezzar's vision in Daniel 2 describes the progress of world history through the Babylonian, Medo-Persian, Greek, and Roman empires. Each empire is represented by a piece of a statue made from different elements. In the end, the entire statue is smashed by a rock, but not one cut by human hands. The rock grew into a mountain and filled the whole world while the statue became a pile of shattered fragments that the wind blew away without leaving a trace (Dan 2:35). So it will be with my American citizenship, as well as the citizenship of every British, German, French, Chinese, Argentinian, and Japanese Christian. Those allegiances will be swallowed up in our eternal citizenship. Our application of today's meditation is to set our hearts more fully on heaven than on earth, to not be more American (or German, or British, or Chinese, etc.) than we are Christian. Our true citizenship is in heaven.

PRAY

Lord Jesus, you are my king. Your kingdom is my true home. I am truly grateful for the advantages of my earthly citizenship, but I am aware as Paul says here that my true citizenship is in heaven. Help me to live accordingly. Help me to set my heart fully on you, Christ, and your coming glory. Amen.

STUDY IT FURTHER

1. Why do you think the tribune in Acts 22 felt it was worth it to have paid a huge sum for his Roman citizenship? How did Paul occasionally use the benefits of his Roman citizenship? What are some of the benefits of your earthly citizenship now? How are all of those earthly benefits nothing compared to the benefits of our citizenship in heaven?

2. Do you think patriotism is a good thing? If so, why? How can it be beneficial in the Christian life? How could it become a problem? What might idolizing citizenship in

one's earthly country look like? Have there been examples of nationalism getting in the way of a healthy Christian life?

3. Do you agree that there will be no patriotism in heaven? Why or why not?

Day 30

Philippians 3:21

READ

[Jesus Christ] will transform our lowly body to be like his glorious body, by the power that enables him even to subject all things to himself.

MEDITATE

What an awesome hope the Lord has bought for us by his death and mighty resurrection. This one verse captures the hope that should be burning in the heart of every child of God—our resurrection from the dead. As we saw in our last study, Paul says we are awaiting the second coming of Christ, looking forward every day to that moment when he will end all human history and usher in the kingdom of God, of which we are all truly citizens. But today's verse shows the transformation that must happen in each of us to enable us to live forever in that coming world. Our lowly bodies must be transformed, conformed to Christ's glorious body. When Paul says, "lowly body," he is speaking of this present physical body, which is under the death sentence in Adam. It is a "mortal body" (Rom 8:11), meaning it is dying and will die. As we age in this world, we see the effects of Adam's sin both in us and around us. We see the ravages of disease, injury, and aging. We know we are in bondage to decay like the entire physical world around us. If we are not part of the final generation, we will most certainly die. Our corpses will be buried into the cold earth where corruption will destroy them completely—microbes and worms will devour all but the bones. In 1 Corinthians 15:42–44, Paul captures well the attributes of our "lowly bodies" at their worst—as lifeless corpses that are sown in the earth: corrupt, weak, dishonored, natural. But by glorious contrast, in that same passage he describes our resurrection bodies with these words: incorruptible, powerful, glorious, and spiritual.

That is what we will have when Christ transforms our lowly bodies and conforms them to his own glorious body. Imagine what it will be like in heaven when our salvation is at last complete. Then God's eternal purpose to conform all his elect children to the image of his Son (Rom 8:29) will at last be consummated. We will run and never grow weary; we will walk and never grow faint (Isa 40:31). We will never get sick, experience pain, or die again (Rev 21:4). We will shine like the sun in the kingdom of our Father (Matt 13:44). I don't think we can meditate too much on this glorious transformation that will most certainly come at the end of the world. It should fill us with power and hope this very day. Paul speaks of eagerly awaiting the coming of the Savior (Phil 3:20). That is hope, our bright Christian hope. Given that we are surrounded by people who are living for their bellies and who have no such hope (see v. 19), our open and eager anticipation of this future will make some of them ask us to give a reason for the hope we so evidently have (1 Pet 3:15).

REFLECT ON CHRIST

Paul says this transformation of our lowly bodies into conformity with Christ's glorious body is a display of Christ's power over everything. By his sovereign power, Christ is able to subdue all things to himself, Paul says. Christ's power is not evident to everyone now; we see it only by faith, but "all authority in heaven and on earth" has been given to him (Matt 28:18). Paul said that Christ is presently and gradually subduing all his enemies one by one, and the last enemy to be subdued is death (1 Cor 15:29). When he comes in glory, he will call forth from the tombs all of his dead people with a mighty voice of power; all who are in their graves will hear his voice and come out (John 5:25), and those who are righteous by faith in Christ will come out into his resurrection glory to shine "like the brightness of the sky above" (Dan 12:3). Then "the power that enables him even to subject all things to himself" will be clearly manifest to both his people and his enemies alike.

APPLY GOD'S WORD

Meditate on what your resurrection body will be like. Think about the four descriptions of that body in 1 Corinthians 15:42–44: incorruptible, powerful, glorious, and spiritual. Let this concept drive away any sorrow you have over your present circumstances—your pains, your diseases, your injuries, your aging. Understand that God's planned salvation for you, total conformity to the image of his Son, includes this conformity to his glorious body. Let that hope fill your heart. Speak to a lost person today about these themes. Ask him/her, "What do you think happens after death?" or "Are you afraid to die?" Then see where the conversation goes. Soon you will be able to articulate your hope from this very passage. It may be the moment of salvation for your lost friend.

PRAY

Heavenly Father, I see the ravages of sin and death around me every day, and I feel them in my own lowly body. Yet I know that someday you will give me a body as glorious as that of your Son. Fill me with that hope right now. And then, give me a chance to speak to a lost person today who sees me so radiant with hope and asks me why I am so hopeful. Amen.

STUDY IT FURTHER

1. What is the significance of Paul saying that "flesh and blood cannot inherit the kingdom of God" and that "the perishable cannot inherit the imperishable" (1 Cor 15:50)? If our bodies could age in heaven, how would it be impossible for us to enjoy heaven?

2. Revelation 22:2 says the leaves of the tree of life are for the healing of the nations. Since there will never be any more death, mourning, crying, or pain in heaven (Rev 21:4), how do you understand the leaves administering healing?

3. We have walked through 1 Corinthians 15:42–44 before. What aspect of the four things said about our resurrection bodies most excites you? How could a vibrant hope based on bodily resurrection from the dead give you a platform for witnessing to lost people?

Day 31

Philippians 4:1

READ

Therefore, my brothers, whom I love and long for, my joy and crown, stand firm thus in the Lord, my beloved.

MEDITATE

This verse sums up all that Paul has been saying about the Christian life in Philippians 3. First, remember that Paul has been strongly advocating an energetic, passionate, relentless pursuit of knowing Christ: "forgetting what lies behind and straining forward to what lies ahead, I press on toward the goal for the prize of the upward call of God in Christ Jesus" (Phil 3:13–14). That entire journey was nothing less than knowing Christ more and more—both in spiritual power and in physical suffering. Only that relentless pursuit will lead to the goal of salvation, the resurrection of the body from the dead, and our lowly bodies being transformed and conformed to Christ's glorious body (3:21). The call is to move forward, race, and pursue Christ every day of your life.

Here Paul commands the Philippians (and therefore all of us): "Stand firm thus in the Lord, my beloved" (4:1). "Thus" means "in this manner" or "this is how" you *stand fast* in the Lord. To *stand fast* is static. Paul uses this stationary language often when exhorting Christians. He calls on the Ephesians to be "rooted and grounded in love" (Eph 3:17). He commands the Colossians to continue in the faith, "stable and steadfast, not shifting from the hope of the gospel that you heard" (Col 1:23). So, which is it? Are we to stand firm (static), or are we to make relentless progress (dynamic)?

There are two ways to understand this static and dynamic view of the Christian life. In the first place, it comes back to the difference between justification and sanctification. Justification is a once-for-all declaration by God that we are forgiven of all sins, righteous in his sight, holy and blameless in Christ. That cannot be improved on and will never be taken from us. It is the unshakeable ground under our feet, the solid rock of Christ's love for us. By it we can make relentless progress toward actual holiness in mind and life. God declares that we *are* holy positionally, so therefore we can *become* holy practically. In the second place, it relates to unchanging doctrinal truths in God's word and the application of those truths to our growing souls. By standing firm on God's immutable word, we make relentless progress toward God's Son.

An image that helps me is of a climber making the final ascent to the summit of Mount Everest, climbing with rugged determination step by step along the icy edge with his steel crampons dug solidly into the mountain. He must progress to reach the highest point on planet earth, but, every step of the way, crosswinds of gale force threaten to sweep him from the mountain. He must keep going but also be firmly planted on the mountain every step of the way.

REFLECT ON CHRIST

Both static and dynamic views of the Christian life ultimately come down to Christ Jesus. In Christ's finished work on the cross and the empty tomb, all Christians find the solid rock of God's unchanging love and purpose for them. Christ died for sin, once for all, making us holy by his blood (Heb 10:10). Christ rose from the dead, once for all, to give us life, and he cannot ever die again (Rom 6:9). These historical facts can never change, and they give us an unchanging hope in an ever-changing world. God set his love on us in Christ once for all and that can never be altered—it can never increase, and it will never decrease. The static truths of the gospel all come down to Christ, forever and ever.

As well, the dynamic view of the Christian life comes down to Christ. Knowing Christ and becoming like him is the relentless goal of every day. In heaven, though all darkness will have been purged forever from both our bodies and our souls and we will be perfectly like Christ, we will forever be learning new aspects of his glory. In Christ are hidden all the treasures of wisdom and knowledge (Col 2:3). Therefore, our education in Christ's infinite person will only have just begun when we are raised from the dead into heavenly glory. As God reveals more and more of his Son to us in the heavenly assembly, we will again and again fall on our faces and worship him, casting our crowns of earthly achievement before his throne (Rev 4:9–11). The heavenly "whenever" in Revelation 4:9 implies a dynamic heaven in which wave upon wave of new insights about Christ will result in more and more opportunities to cast our crowns in worship. Paul calls the Philippians his "joy and crown." It is the greatest achievement of his life to win souls for heaven. But whatever was to Paul's glory, he will gladly cast before the feet of the Savior again and again, giving him full credit. We will never cease learning and giving Christ all glory.

APPLY GOD'S WORD

Paul commands us to "stand firm thus in the Lord." Stand firm in the unchanging truths of the gospel so that you can make relentless progress in Christ. Feed your soul with his unchanging word, then pursue knowing Christ with relentless passion. The static is the basis for the dynamic—all is in Christ and for his glory. Do it today, by the power of the Holy Spirit.

PRAY

Thank you, Father, that you have put an unchanging rock under my feet—Christ's finished work at the cross and the tomb. Help me to be rooted and established in the love of Christ at the cross and in his resurrection glory, so that today I can grow in grace and the knowledge of Christ. Amen.

STUDY IT FURTHER

1. Hebrews 4:12 says God's word is "living and active." But Psalm 119:89 says God's word is "firmly fixed in the heavens." Jesus said, "Heaven and earth will pass away, but my words will not pass away" (Matt 24:35). How is God's word both dynamic and unchanging?

2. How does the permanent truth of our justification help fuel relentless growth in Christlikeness? How does stability promote change?

3. Indications are that the saints in heaven will be both totally perfect but also constantly learning new aspects of God's glory. How does that make heaven both a stable and dynamic place?

Day 32

Philippians 4:2–3

READ

I entreat Euodia and I entreat Syntyche to agree in the Lord. Yes, I ask you also, true companion, help these women, who have labored side by side with me in the gospel together with Clement and the rest of my fellow workers, whose names are in the book of life.

MEDITATE

It is amazing how much God has accomplished in building his kingdom with such inferior building materials as ourselves. Here Paul is begging two servants of the Lord, Euodia and Syntyche, to get along with each other. They both love the Lord and labored side by side with Paul in the work of the gospel. They bowed in faith before the cross of Christ, received the same pardon for their sins, were adopted into the same spiritual family, were indwelt with the same Spirit, read the same Scriptures, and had the same hope in heaven as each other. But it seems they bicker and argue and fall into strife whenever they are together. So much so that Paul has to beg them to be of the same mind in the Lord, including their strife in this beautiful epistle to the entire church. He even appeals to a person he calls "true companion" to help these women come to unity in Jesus.

We have already seen that Christian unity is based on the Trinity, a perfect unity of mind, affections, and will. In Philippians 2:1–4, Paul laid out that pattern as the standard for all Christian fellowship. It is achieved only when Christians have the same mind as Christ, a mind of total humility in servanthood to others for the glory of God (Phil 2:5–11). When the mind of Christ has taken hold of them, they will truly humble themselves before each other and consider the other person better than themselves and the other person's interests as more important than their own (Phil 2:4). Clearly neither Euodia nor Syntyche were doing that, and their shameful spat has been immortalized in the pages of holy Scripture.

Yet God uses imperfect sinners to do eternally glorious things in building the kingdom of Christ. All of us are weak and selfish, struggling with fleshly pride. Sometimes we need help from other Christians to resolve bitter conflicts. The sooner we come to that sweet Trinitarian unity that we will experience forever in heaven, the better. Most local churches are from time to time torn apart and rendered ineffective for the gospel because of human conflict. The same is sadly true with every mission agency. The most common reason that missionaries quit the field and return to their native land is conflict with other missionaries. Euodia and Syntyche have had two thousand years of spiritual descendants who have wasted time in conflict with each other rather than focusing on pure spiritual warfare against their own sins and in rescuing the lost from Satan's dark kingdom.

REFLECT ON CHRIST

We already know the answer to Christian conflict: "Have this mind among yourselves, which is yours in Christ Jesus"

(Phil 2:5). Imitating the perfect humility and servanthood of Christ frees us from the pride and sinful anger that shreds sweet Christian fellowship. The power to love a brother or sister in the midst of a disagreement, to see that person as holy in Christ, to see their future in heaven perfectly conformed to Christ, and to realize that we will spend eternity in heaven in absolute agreement about everything, this has the power to dissolve conflict among Christians and to restore unity in the Spirit.

Vital to this is realizing that it is possible now to be of the same mind in the Lord. We actually can come to full agreement right now by the Spirit of Christ. It takes humility, prayer, talking and (more importantly) listening, and time. Genuine agreement in the Lord is one of the birthrights we all share in the Spirit.

APPLY GOD'S WORD

Are you in conflict with a Christian right now? Perhaps arguments are hurting your marriage. Perhaps there is a fellow church member with whom you are consistently butting heads. Total agreement in the Lord is possible and well worth pursuing. Make the time to meet with that person and tell him/her your goal: unity in mind and heart—heavenly agreement. Believe that in every complex issue you are trying to resolve, God is working in each of you that you may humbly work together. Since you understand your own viewpoint better than the other's, humbly ask them to share their insights. Ask sincere questions to probe the dimensions of their perspective. Seek the Lord's truth in what they are saying as much as possible. Hopefully, the other person will be inspired to do the same with you. In this pattern, you may together arrive at a solution in which each person contributed and God was glorified.

Or it may be that you are not personally involved in the conflict. Perhaps you are the "true companion" that the Spirit of Christ is enlisting (as Paul did) to bring about genuine reconciliation and like-mindedness among two choice servants of the Lord. Follow the pattern we have discussed here. God can use flawed, sinful servants like us to do eternally glorious things for Christ's kingdom. Let him use you.

PRAY

Father, it is with shame that we must confess how argumentative we are. Two thousand years of church history has been ripped apart by one prideful disagreement after another. Forgive us, Lord! Make us truly humble, truly one with each other. Amen.

STUDY IT FURTHER

1. How do you see strife between the Lord's servants as a key obstacle to the growth of the kingdom of Christ? Read John 17:23. How does the growth of genuine unity between the Lord's disciples affect their witness in the world?

2. Read Ephesians 2:14–16. Paul is talking about Jew-Gentile unity, but we know that there are all kinds of groups all over the world that, apart from Christ, hate each other and are at enmity with each other. How can a surprising unity between people of rival factions be a powerful force in spreading the gospel of Christ?

3. Where do you see strife in your own life? In your marriage? Family? Church? Neighborhood? Workplace? How can these principles of love and unity help?

Day 33

Philippians 4:4

READ

Rejoice in the Lord always; again I will say, rejoice.

MEDITATE

Paul commands every generation of Christians to "rejoice in the Lord." Therefore it is vital for Christians to refuse to surrender to deep depression as though there can be no answer suitable to the sorrows they face. The source of the rejoicing is not in the circumstances but in the Lord—that is, in Jesus Christ crucified, resurrected, gloriously reigning, who will triumph by his Spirit every day of redemptive history and who will return in glory to reign forever. This attitude in the Christian life is so vital that Paul says it for the second time in this epistle (see 3:1) and then immediately repeats it in this verse: "again I will say, rejoice."

Jesus is the eternal joy-giver. Though sin and death entered the world, and as a result, every generation of humanity has had to sail through a sea of incalculable sorrow, Jesus entered the world to rescue us and bring us to a world of perfect joy. Jesus spoke of the joy that would fill the hearts of his disciples when he had conquered death and rose triumphantly from the grave. He likened it to the joy that a woman has in labor and childbirth. She writhes in anguish and cries aloud in agony, but once the child is born, she no longer remembers the anguish because of the joy that a child is born into the world. "So also you have sorrow now, but I will see you again, and your hearts will rejoice, and no one will take your joy from you" (John 16:21–22). In heaven, all the redeemed will be swimming in an endless sea of the glory of God. We will be eternally learning new aspects of the infinite greatness of God, and each new vision of his glory will bring shouts of praise from the countless multitude of the redeemed. How can any words I write even come close to capturing the pulses and surges of joy we will feel at that time? "Now we see in a mirror dimly, but then face to face" (1 Cor 13:12). Nevertheless, the more we meditate on Scripture's descriptions of heaven's joys, the more we will live victorious and fruitful Christian lives now.

The world, the flesh, and the devil will constantly conspire to kill our joy. Our job is to fight back. We must be transformed by the renewing of our minds (Rom 12:2) so that we see afresh every day how magnificent are the person and work of Christ and how glorious are his promises. We must not let our flesh and the world lure us toward carnal "joys" that are deceptive and poisonous. We must take up the shield of faith to extinguish all the flaming arrows of Satan—his temptations and accusations—that are designed to steal our joy. And then, we must let our joy be evident to everyone we know.

REFLECT ON CHRIST

This joy in the Lord is a Christ-centered joy, flowing from the infinite perfections of his person and the astonishing achievements of his life. Go over the attributes of Christ on display in the four Gospel accounts. Read of his power in driving out demons effortlessly with a mere word. Read of his skill in healing every disease and sickness among the people. Read of the clear display of his deity in stilling the storm. Read of the compassion of his heart in touching the leper (Mark 1) and raising the only son of the widow of Nain (Luke 7). Read of his amazing wisdom in the Sermon on the Mount and the extended teachings in John's Gospel—the bread of life (John 6) and the good shepherd (John 10). Read of his staggering courage in agreeing in Gethsemane to drink the cup of wrath his Father offered him. Read of his perfect obedience in dying on the cross for our sins. Then read the accounts of his resurrection from the dead, how he showed the disciples his hands and his side as clear evidence of his victory. But best of all, read these accounts in light of his gospel promises to you—full forgiveness of sins, your own glorious resurrection from the grave patterned after his, and your eternal inheritance in heaven. As you read all these things by faith, you will find your joy in the Lord surging in renewed power. Then remind yourself the next day and the next of Christ's redeeming power.

APPLY GOD'S WORD

When you have done all the practical things I suggested in the last paragraph, get ready to fight all day long that your joy may not die. There is no witness so powerful in this dying world as that of joy-filled Christians. It is vital for us to maintain our joy in the Lord no matter what happens today. Trials will come to test your joy. Be strong in the Lord and refuse to allow your joy to leak out. As you walk in this evident and supernatural joy, ask God to use you to bring hope to someone who is lost, who may ask you why you are so consistently filled with joy. Then you will have the privilege to show them the source of your fountain: the person and work of Christ. If they listen and trust Christ, your joy on earth will find its infinitely superior echo in heaven, for God will celebrate before the angels the salvation of one more of his elect.

PRAY

Father, how can we thank you enough for all the joy we have in this world because of your Son? Please enable my joy to grow. Take away any earthly sorrow that is presently attacking my joy in the Lord. Help me to give you these burdens and allow your joy in me to be maintained by your Spirit. Amen.

STUDY IT FURTHER

1. Read Isaiah 9:2–7. What aspects of that prophecy point toward "rejoicing in the Lord always"?

2. Paul speaks of himself in 2 Corinthians 6:10 as "sorrowful, yet always rejoicing." How should we understand that concept? How can we be both sorrowful and rejoicing in the Lord?

3. How can meditating on the heavenly glory in Revelation 21–22 help increase your joy?

Day 34

Philippians 4:5

READ

Let your gentleness be evident to all. The Lord is near. (NIV)

MEDITATE

We live in an increasingly harsh society. People are angry, prideful, and rude to each other. They tear savagely into total strangers on social media if they have different views. They drive with murderous rage. They delight in movies that celebrate revenge and vigilante justice. Acid drops from their tongues, burning the hearts of those they attack. In all of this, they do not know that they are behaving just like their father, the devil, who is filled with rage because he knows his time is short (Rev 12:12). When they speak harsh words, they are speaking his language because their hearts are conformed to his.

But Christians are called to an entirely different standard. Paul commands us to be famous for gentleness. The word he uses here for gentleness gives a sense of reasonableness, mildness, or kindness, and it implies restraint—a withholding of the power to injure so that we may benefit others. Paul says this character trait should be so obvious in our lives that anyone who knows us would think of this immediately. To earn this status, we must deny ourselves on many occasions, be forgiving of all grievances, and purposely choose mild and pleasant words, especially when we have been wronged.

The clearest example of this trait, of course, is our Lord Jesus Christ. Let's spend more time meditating on his example so we can imitate him.

REFLECT ON CHRIST

Paul says the reason we should let our gentleness be evident to all is that "the Lord is near." It is possible he meant that the Lord is near as a judge who sees everything we do and will call us to account for how we treat others, but I think it more likely that Paul conceives of this nearness as the immediate presence of the Lord by his Spirit to help us be as gentle as he was.

The gentleness of Jesus was more than just known to all men while he ministered among the people. He earned that reputation by his selfless healings of countless suffering people who waited all day to be touched by him. He was especially gentle to women and children. The woman who had suffered twelve years of bleeding and who anonymously touched the hem of his garment out of shame felt his gentleness when he said to her, "Take heart, daughter; your faith has made you well" (Matt 9:22). Jairus's daughter felt his gentleness when Jesus took her by the hand and said, "Little girl, I say to you, arise" (Mark 5:41). The terrified townspeople of the Gerasenes who begged Jesus to leave their region after he had driven out the legion of demons from the man felt his gentleness when he meekly got back into the boat to leave (Mark 5:18). The children who gathered around him felt his gentleness when he took them in his arms and blessed them (Mark 10:16). The widow at Nain who was burying her only son felt his gentleness when he said to her, "Do not weep" (Luke 7:13). The centurion who nailed him to the cross felt his gentleness when he said, "Father, forgive them, for they know not what they do" (Luke 23:34). And the thief on the cross, who had earlier reviled Jesus but then repented and asked to be welcomed into his kingdom, felt his gentleness when he said, "Today you will be with me in paradise" (Luke 23:43).

Isaiah foresaw the gentleness of Jesus in dealing with brokenhearted sinners when he prophesied, "A bruised reed he will not break and a faintly burning wick he will not quench" (Isa 42:3). Bruised reeds are weak plants, hanging by a slender green thread. Jesus skillfully and gently binds them back together and gives them life, then transforms them and strengthens them. Smoldering wicks are just about to go out. Jesus skillfully and gently nurses their spark into a roaring fire of righteousness. This is the gentle but sustaining power of Jesus.

The only description Jesus ever gave of himself is this: "I am gentle and lowly in heart" (Matt 11:29). That gentleness is powerfully attractive to all sinners, for Jesus also says, "Come to me, all you who labor and are heavy laden, and I will give you rest" (Matt 11:28). Christ's gentleness saves our souls, and this is the very gentleness that Paul commands all Christians to display as well.

APPLY GOD'S WORD

This command from the Lord to all Christians is one of the sweetest we can obey. It frees us from bitterness and the trail of wreckage that results from living life on an angry rampage. It causes us to respond with kindness to people who have harshly mistreated us, and it gives us a platform from which to proclaim the gospel of a gentle Savior who is ready to cover all the sins of those who come to him. Each of us can obey this command by the power of the Holy Spirit. Ask the Lord to make you a gentle person today. Ask him to correct your habits of harshness, whether in language, or while driving, or in the workplace, or when wronged, to habits of grace.

PRAY

Lord Jesus, you are gentle and lowly of heart, and you know all my sins. You know that I have pridefully and angrily lived a life of harshness in many settings. Please forgive me. Please work a transformation in me by your Spirit. Amen.

STUDY IT FURTHER

1. At Jesus's baptism, the Holy Spirit descended as a dove. How does the dove represent the gentleness of the Holy Spirit? How does the fruit of the Spirit in Galatians 5:22–23 tend toward gentleness, especially "self-control"?

2. Read Richard Sibbes's classic *The Bruised Reed* (it's freely available online). Ask the Lord to give you a deeper sense of the gentleness of Christ as Sibbes unfolds it.

3. How could understanding the gentleness of Christ in dealing with sinners help us to be more gracious with lost people we know?

Day 35

Philippians 4:6–7

READ

Do not be anxious about anything, but in everything by prayer and supplication with thanksgiving let your requests be made known to God. And the peace of God, which surpasses all understanding, will guard your hearts and your minds in Christ Jesus.

MEDITATE

Anxiety is a devastating use of a marvelous gift from God—our imaginations. By our imaginations, we ponder the future and can see things that don't yet exist as though they did. By this gift, we can dream up new inventions, write novels, come up with new therapies for diseases, and sketch out the framework and details of a better world. But by it we can also become enslaved to the terrors of worst-case scenarios. Most of these scenarios never come to pass, but the anxieties they breed enslave our minds to fear while our imaginations color in the details.

Anxiety is the opposite of hope. Hope is a feeling in the heart that the future is bright based on the promises of God. Anxiety is a feeling in the heart that the future is dark based on our own imaginations. In today's passage, God calls all Christians to fight anxiety with prayer, and this call is absolute and comprehensive. He commands us not to be anxious about *anything* but give *everything* to God in prayer. There should be no earthly outcome that enslaves the heart of any Christian to fear. Jesus certainly warned us, "In this world you will have trouble" (John 16:33 NIV). I know that loved ones may well get sick and die. I am aware that natural disasters may well destroy our homes. I have seen many years of pain and sorrow in my life and the lives of those around me. I know we live in a world cursed by God through Adam's sin. But I also know that "all things work together for good to those who love God, to those who are the called according to his purpose" (Rom 8:28 NKJV). God has taught me that only by "various trials" can my faith be brought to full maturity in this world (Jas 1:2–4). Therefore, I must learn to take all my fears of negative outcomes to God in prayer.

The remedy to anxiety is prayer and supplication with thanksgiving. Bring your requests to God. Tell him all about them. Pour out your heart's deepest concerns and highest aspirations to God in prayer. Prayer is overt dependence on God; prayerlessness is sinful independence from God. As the hymn, "What a Friend We Have in Jesus," puts it, "We should never be discouraged; take it to the Lord in prayer."

This command comes with the sweetest possible promise: the "peace of God, which surpasses all understanding, will guard your hearts and mind through Christ Jesus." God is a God of peace. Nothing ruffles him or confuses him or surprises him. "Our God is in the heavens; he does all that he pleases" (Ps 115:3). This is the "peace of God." He promises to give it to you if you pray. It is a supernatural peace, one that surpasses all understanding, meaning you don't fully understand why you feel so peaceful when so many terrible things are happening.

God hasn't explained all the details of his plan to you, yet you still feel peaceful. And that peace is standing guard over your heart and mind—like Job's "hedge of protection" from the Lord (Job 1:10), not allowing any dark thought to sneak in and assassinate your peace.

REFLECT ON CHRIST

This peace of God that surpasses all understanding does its guardian work over your heart and mind "through Christ Jesus." The sublime power and peaceful demeanor of Jesus Christ is the source of that supernatural peace. Picture yourself in the boat with the disciples when the storm swept over the Sea of Galilee, causing the breakers to swell and the boat to sink. Jesus was asleep in the stern, lying peacefully on a cushion. You are a veteran fisherman from Galilee, and you have been in many storms. You choose to let Jesus keep sleeping while you do all that your skills and experience have taught you to do. You sail this way or that. You row with all your might. You bail and bail and bail. You let Jesus sleep because, after all, what does he know about boats and the sea? This is your wheelhouse. But the circumstances overwhelm you, and it becomes clear the boat is about to be swamped entirely. Finally, you wake Jesus with the strange words, "Teacher, don't you care that we are perishing?" (Mark 4:38). You never expected what happens next. Jesus merely speaks to the wind and the waves, saying, "Peace, be still," and the storm instantly ends. As you look back on the event years later, you realize something powerful. Jesus knows more about everything than you do—including handling a boat on the Sea of Galilee. Your biggest mistake that day was that you turned to him last rather than first. You prayed at the end, when all your personal resources were exhausted. Next time, you will bring him in at the very beginning of every trial.

This is the peace of God that will guard your heart and mind in Christ Jesus.

APPLY GOD'S WORD

The application is simple and clear: take everything to the Lord in prayer. Pray longer, pray in more detail, pray with more faith. As soon as any circumstance comes that can rob you of peace, take it to the Lord in prayer. Extend your prayer life—further and further—until you are living constantly under a shelter of supernatural peace spun thread by thread in prayer. Prayerlessness may be the most under-addressed sin of the Christian life. When we get to Judgment Day and review our lives, we will have no answer to the Lord's repeated question to us, "Why didn't you bring it to me in prayer?" There will be no redeeming answer at that time because the answer is clear, as it was for the fishermen on the Sea of Galilee—self-reliance. Repent today of self-reliance and pray longer and in more detail for every circumstance that might cause you anxiety.

PRAY

Gracious God, you have commanded us to draw near to your throne of grace for help in time of need. Every moment is a time of need. Forgive me for my anxieties. Forgive me also for my self-reliance and prayerlessness. Work in me a spirit of prayer such as I have never displayed before. Amen.

STUDY IT FURTHER

1. Read Matthew 6:25–34. Walk through the reasons Jesus gives there against all anxiety. Also make note of his various remedies for faithless anxiety.

2. George Mueller ran a system of orphanages that cared for over ten thousand orphans in his lifetime. He kept a detailed prayer journal, which recorded over fifty thousand specific answers to prayer. Do some research on Mueller's prayer journals to find some inspiring examples of specific answers to prayer.

3. How can studying great prayer warriors of church history help you grow in the spiritual discipline of driving out faithless anxiety by effectual, fervent prayer?

Day 36

Philippians 4:8–9

READ

Finally, brothers, whatever is true, whatever is honorable, whatever is just, whatever is pure, whatever is lovely, whatever is commendable, if there is any excellence, if there is anything worthy of praise, think about these things. What you have learned and received and heard and seen in me—practice these things, and the God of peace will be with you.

MEDITATE

I have visited some great battlefields in my life. I have seen Yorktown, where our nation's freedom from British rule was won. I have seen Lexington and Concord, where war was started in fire and blood. I have seen Gettysburg, where over 51,000 men died or were injured in the greatest battle ever fought on American soil. As significant as all these battlefields are, they pale in comparison with the most significant battlefield in history: the human mind. From the temptation of Adam and Eve in the garden of Eden until this very day, God and Satan have waged an unequal battle for control of the thoughts of people. This invisible battlefield is described in many places in Scripture.

Paul says that before we were converted "we all once lived in the passions of our flesh, carrying out the desires of the body *and the mind*, and were by nature children of wrath" (Eph 2:3, italics added). He says in Romans 8:5–7 that the mind controlled by the flesh is death, but the mind controlled by the Spirit is life and peace. Conversion occurs when God transforms our minds and hearts by his Spirit through the gospel of Jesus Christ. Even after this transformation, there is still a battle for control of our minds because the thoughts of the mind dictate the actions of the body. Galatians 5:17 says that the flesh lusts against the Spirit and the Spirit against the flesh; there is a constant internal warfare for control of the mind and therefore of the person.

The remedy is mind-control by the Spirit with the pattern of thinking dictated by the words of Scripture. Some people think they cannot control their thought-life, but today's text tells us directly what to meditate on. We are in charge of what we meditate on. No, we cannot keep Satan from hurling flaming thought arrows at us, but we can control what we focus on and ponder. Paul commands us to fix our thoughts on "whatever things are true ... honorable ... just ... pure ... lovely ... commendable," excellent, praiseworthy. Think about these things and only these things.

Scripture feeds us a steady diet of many things in each of these delightful categories: true as opposed to false doctrine or the lies of the Evil One; honorable as opposed to depraved or disgusting; just or righteous as opposed to unjust or unrighteous; pure as opposed to defiled; lovely as opposed to ugly; commendable as opposed to shameful; excellent as opposed to degraded; praiseworthy as opposed to worthy of condemnation. Satan, by his constant assault on our senses through his darkly brilliant world system of lusts, wants to drag our thoughts into the gutter. It is truly disgusting what we will do in our minds. How ashamed would we be to have a week's worth of our thoughts portrayed on a screen at church. God calls us to lift our minds from the darkness to the light.

Beyond this, in verse 9, Paul presents himself as a role model for the Christian life. The very thing he mentioned back in 3:17 is restated here. We do a lot of our learning by watching Christian leaders put into practice the doctrines they have absorbed into their hearts. Paul was one of the greatest role models the church has ever seen, and he promised that if the Philippians imitated him, the God of peace would be with them.

REFLECT ON CHRIST

The text calls us to meditate and gives us a series of descriptions of the kinds of spiritually beautiful things worthy of our constant thoughts. Some time ago, I realized that Jesus Christ is the incarnation of all these attributes. Jesus Christ is true, honorable, just, pure, lovely, commendable, excellent, and praiseworthy. Choose any one of these words and line it up with Christ as he is portrayed in Scripture and you will see the perfect match. Jesus is the embodiment of truth itself, for he said, "I am ... the truth" (John 14:6). He doesn't merely speak the truth, or commend the truth to us, or live according to the truth; he is truth incarnate. The same is true of the word honorable. What does it mean for a man to be "honorable"? Is it to act courageously with virtuous goals? No one has ever been more honorable than Jesus. What about "just" or "righteous"? Jesus lived out perfect righteousness at every moment of his life, and he has become our righteousness in the sight of God (1 Cor 1:30).

Every beautiful word Paul lays out for us to ponder finds its perfection in Christ. This is especially true of Christ on the cross, the greatest single display of the glory of God in the history of the world. Ponder continually Christ crucified and you will fulfill Paul's command for a pure thought life.

APPLY GOD'S WORD

You may think that this kind of mind control is not possible, but God's word is perfect and cannot mislead us. If this is commanded, then the Holy Spirit is able to work it out in our lives. We should follow his leading to a pure mind (Rom 8:14). A practical step is the consistent intake of the word of God, beginning with daily time immersed in Scripture. This devotional in Philippians is a guided daily meditation on text after text of this epistle, but you need to go beyond this book to your own broader and deeper meditations on Scripture. No discipline I have ever embraced has been more effective for controlling my thought life than the extended memorization of Scripture. Why not challenge yourself to memorize the whole book of Philippians? It is 104 verses, and at a verse a day, you could have it hidden in your heart less than four months from now. In any case, the best application of this passage is to think constantly about your glorious Savior, Jesus Christ. Read the Gospels and take up a moment in Christ's life every day, pondering it and saturating your mind with it.

In addition to the good food of the word, resolve not to fill your mind with low, corrupt, vile, worldly images and concepts. Protect your thought life by refusing to feed it the garbage the world delights in.

PRAY

Father, our whole bodies are fearfully and wonderfully made, but no part is more complex or astonishing than our minds. You created us in your image, and that is especially displayed in our ability to think, to reason, to ponder, to understand, to love, to hate, to rejoice, to mourn, to choose. God transform me by the renewing of my mind. Make me think only godly thoughts. Amen.

STUDY IT FURTHER

1. Psalm 1:1–3 commends the richness of a life spent meditating day and night on God's word. Memorize these three verses and meditate on them all day today. See what blessing will come into your life.

2. Go online and find a copy of my booklet, *An Approach to the Extended Memorization of Scripture*. Read it and ask the Lord if he would have you memorize Philippians.

3. How can pondering on the person of Christ help you fulfill this command about your thought life?

Day 37

Philippians 4:10–12

READ

I rejoiced in the Lord greatly that now at length you have revived your concern for me. You were indeed concerned for me, but you had no opportunity. Not that I am speaking of being in need, for I have learned in whatever situation I am to be content. I know how to be brought low, and I know how to abound. In any and every circumstance, I have learned the secret of facing plenty and hunger, abundance and need.

MEDITATE

This passage (especially 4:11–13) is what preacher Jeremiah Burroughs called "the rare jewel of Christian contentment." Few topics in the Christian life, when mastered, can bring as much fruit in the present world as contentment. What is contentment? The basic idea is one of happy fulfillment, a combination of joy and peace based on fullness or satisfaction. Picture a family an hour after a Thanksgiving feast, when everyone is warm and full and happy. The concept here is vastly higher than that, however. The Greek word Paul uses for Christian contentment is best translated "self-sufficiency," literally being supplied from self and not from any outside source. This concept understood wrongly would imply the very sort of independence from God that salvation is meant to cure. Paul said in 2 Corinthians 1:8–9 that God had orchestrated a bitter trial to teach him not to trust in himself but in God who raises the dead. Jesus said, "I am the vine; you are the branches. Whoever abides in me and I in him, he it is that bears much fruit, for apart from me you can do nothing" (John 15:5). Clearly Christian contentment does not violate that basic principle of salvation. I think "self-sufficient" here really means "God-sufficient." It is like God in relation to his creation: God needs nothing from creation for his essential existence. God is independent of all creatures; he existed before all of them and needs nothing from them to continue to exist. Christian contentment is a mysterious drawing into the same principle whereby a Christian doesn't really need anything whatsoever from the physical universe—Christ is everything and supplies everything.

Paul and Silas gave the most powerful display of Christian contentment in Philippi when they sang at midnight in the dark, smelly, filthy prison. Their backs were still bleeding, they had had nothing to eat or drink, and they had very dim prospects for the future. Yet their hearts were filled with heavenly joy in Christ and their mouths were filled with song. All the other prisoners were listening to them, and soon God responded with an astonishing precision earthquake—destroying gates and bars and shaking loose chains with not a single injury or death. Soon the Philippian jailer would bring them out and ask, "What must I do to be saved?" That is the power of Christian contentment—the ability to be independent of earthly things and to derive everything from Christ alone. As the psalmist said, "Whom have I in heaven but you? And there is nothing on earth that I desire besides you" (Ps 73:25).

The immediate context of this statement on contentment is Paul's thanks to the Philippians for the money they sent by Epaphroditus. Paul says he rejoiced greatly that they had renewed their care for him by sending their financial support. Paul wanted them to know he is very thankful to them for the money but that his spiritual health did not in any way depend on it. He was content in Christ before the money came, and he would be content in Christ while spending it on his needs, and he would be content in Christ after it was gone. He wanted them to learn the same secret of Christian contentment that he had: in "whatever situation," whether abounding or abased. Paul wants them to have the same joyful freedom of contentment that he had learned, so he uses this occasion as a teaching opportunity.

REFLECT ON CHRIST

Christ is the center of Christian contentment. The fundamental question we must ask in each of our circumstances is this: "Is Christ crucified and resurrected sufficient for me to be joyful right now, or does he have to do more?" Almost certainly, the "more" he would have to do is some earthly thing—some possession, pleasure, position, relationship, or achievement. Perhaps it is something small, some praise from a person who notices the good works we've done. We can get so out of sorts when we serve in some way and a person doesn't thank us. When we are tempted to become discontent at that moment, we must go back to Christ's death on the cross and his triumphant resurrection from the dead. By this all our sins are forgiven, by this we will live forever in a glorious body in a glorious world. Is that enough? Or must we have a little more to push us over the top into true contentment? Christ is everything, or at least he should be.

APPLY GOD'S WORD

This Christian contentment is not guaranteed to all Christians. In verse 12, Paul calls it a secret to be learned. The Greek word translated "I have learned the secret" (*mueō*) was used in mystery religions of the ancient Near East when the advanced practitioners of the mystery religion would know the inner secrets of the shrine or temple and gain spiritual powers. For Paul's use of this word, the secret was learned not in some temple or shrine but in everyday life. For example, Paul learned it in his many imprisonments and daily life experiences. So it is with us. It is eminently possible for a Christian to go through his or her entire life never having learned the secret of Christian contentment: constantly out of sorts and discontent about some earthly thing. In effect, such a person is dragged by the Spirit moaning and groaning, kicking and complaining into heaven. Dear brothers and sisters, don't let this be your attitude in life.

Ask the Lord to teach you this secret. Ask him to use the training of daily life circumstances to teach you to be supernaturally independent of them all, to be equally content in Christ in success or failure, in feasting or fasting, in being praised or being criticized. This is a lifelong journey, but it starts with prayer and a seeking heart: "Lord, teach me to be content in you whatever happens today."

PRAY

Lord, thank you that you are enough for my soul for all eternity. I know it to be true, but I must confess that I don't always live like it. Please teach me the secret of Christian contentment. Amen.

STUDY IT FURTHER

1. Get a copy of Jeremiah Burroughs's classic book *The Rare Jewel of Christian Contentment.* Begin working your way through it. It will greatly strengthen your soul in the area of contentment.

2. Read again the account of Paul and Silas in the Philippian jail (Acts 16). How would you say they displayed Christian contentment there? How does their example strengthen you?

3. Read Numbers 11:1–3. What does that story teach you about how God sees complaining? How is complaining the opposite of Christian contentment?

Day 38

Philippians 4:13

READ

I can do all things through him who strengthens me.

MEDITATE

Christian contentment, we saw yesterday, is a state of joy and peace in Christ independent of all earthly circumstances. It is a secret to be learned, but Paul said he had learned it. Therefore, Christian contentment is possible but not guaranteed. Since this is so, it follows that many Christians live much of their lives in unnecessary patterns of sinful discontentment, missing the rich blessing of the supernatural joy and peace in Christ that enabled Paul and Silas to sing in the Philippian jail.

In *The Rare Jewel of Christian Contentment*, mentioned previously, Jeremiah Burroughs defined contentment as "that sweet, inward, quiet, gracious frame of spirit that freely submits to and delights in God's wise and fatherly disposal in every condition" (p. 19). Let's unpack that. First, contentment is a "frame of spirit," an attitude or mindset, a way of looking at everything, a perspective. Burroughs describes it with four adjectives: sweet (as opposed to bitter or sour), inward (a heart-work, not merely an outward act), quiet (peaceful as opposed to roiling, churning, or contentious), and gracious (that is, worked only by the sovereign grace of God). Second, it is based on God's providence, his decisions about our lives. Burroughs calls it "God's wise and fatherly disposal." God governs our lives as a loving father. He makes decisions about every aspect of our lives, every day of our lives. If we embrace the doctrine of God's providence, his sovereign control over every atom of creation and every second of history, we can learn the secret of Christian contentment. But if we think everything is random, or that God is not acting as a loving father to us, we will never be content. Third, Burroughs says that Christian contentment consists in "freely submitting to and delighting in" every aspect of God's fatherly choices for our lives. We submit to them rather than rebelling against them, and we delight in them because we know that, however painful the circumstances may be, they are part of the wise plan of a loving father for us as his children.

From Burroughs's definition, we are now able to critique our own behavior. Whenever we are discontent, we are essentially rebelling against God's choices for our lives. Then our "frame of spirit" becomes bitter or sour and we become noisy rather than quiet under his mighty and loving hand. We complain against God's choices, murmuring about the weather, or our health, or some financial setback, or some difficult person in our lives. We are so accustomed to this complaining that we scarcely realize what a great sin it really is. Therefore, we must turn away from complaining and ask the Lord to work true contentment in us by his Spirit.

REFLECT ON CHRIST

Paul speaks of Christian contentment as a work of Christ in strengthening the soul: "I can do all things through [Christ] who *strengthens* me." This implies quite plainly that complaining about trials is a display of great weakness. It is a dreadful thing for a Christian to be a chronic complainer. Conversely, it is a display of supernatural power for a Christian to sing in a darkened jail with an empty stomach and a bleeding back. That power comes from Christ alone by his Spirit. If you see yourself in a regular pattern of grumbling against the Lord's providential choices for your life, turn to Christ and ask him to strengthen you. Christ is the perfect display of peaceful submission to the Father's will, for he prayed in Gethsemane, "Not my will, but yours, be done" (Luke 22:42). By his Spirit, Christ lives in you to will and to do according to his good purpose for your life (Phil 2:13). Therefore, the key to Christian contentment in whatever state we find ourselves is drawing close to Christ, abiding in him as a branch does in a vine, and deriving from him continually the life-giving sap we need to rejoice and trust in our Father.

APPLY GOD'S WORD

As with most aspects of the Christian journey, progress toward learning this secret of Christian contentment begins with conviction by the Spirit and confession of sin. We spend a stunning amount of time discontent with our circumstances. We must confess and renounce this sin of discontentment before we can grow. Secondly, we need to immerse ourselves in the doctrine of God's providence, learning from Scripture how true it is that even the very hairs of our head are all numbered and that a sparrow doesn't fall to the ground apart from the sovereign will of God (Matt 10:29–30). Then we need to resolve to be content today by his Spirit, no matter what God brings our way. We need to learn to praise the Lord and thank him for all things, and we need to set our hearts on heaven like never before, knowing that our true joy and fulfillment will never be found in this sin-cursed world. Finally, we need to learn to see every aspect of our earthly lives as a tool in the hands of Christ for the building of his kingdom, not the feathering of a comfortable earthly nest for ourselves. Paul and Silas's contentment in poor circumstances led directly to the Philippian jailer's salvation. Get ready for God to use you to save others.

PRAY

Father, forgive me for my habits of discontentment. Work in me the same Christ-centered peace and joy that Paul and Silas put on display so long ago in that Philippian jail. Amen.

STUDY IT FURTHER

1. How can a supernatural contentment in the midst of an extremely challenging trial be a powerful witness to a lost and dying world? How can you prepare to suffer well (i.e., in a continual display of Christian contentment) before the trial even comes?

2. Read again Jeremiah Burroughs's definition of Christian contentment in today's devotion. What aspect of that definition speaks most powerfully to you today?

3. What circumstances tend to make you the most discontent? How have you seen God help you grow out of those patterns? What tools does the Spirit use most powerfully to bring you to a position of Christian contentment?

Day 39

Philippians 4:14–20

READ

Yet it was kind of you to share my trouble. And you Philippians yourselves know that in the beginning of the gospel, when I left Macedonia, no church entered into partnership with me in giving and receiving, except you only. Even in Thessalonica you sent me help for my needs once and again. Not that I seek the gift, but I seek the fruit that increases to your credit. I have received full payment, and more. I am well supplied, having received from Epaphroditus the gifts you sent, a fragrant offering, a sacrifice acceptable and pleasing to God. And my God will supply every need of yours according to his riches in glory in Christ Jesus. To our God and Father be glory forever and ever. Amen.

MEDITATE

One of the most significant barometers of our spiritual health is how we spend our money. Jesus said more about money than he did about heaven and hell combined. In fact, 15 percent of all of Jesus's words were on this topic.[1] Why? Because money

1. Randy Alcorn, *Money, Possessions and Eternity* (Wheaton, IL: Tyndale, 2003), 4.

is one of the most attractive idols in the world and is in direct conflict with our allegiance to God. To combat this idolatry, Scripture gives us thorough instructions on why and how we should use our money to invest in eternity. This passage is one of the clearest.

The context is the money the Philippians sent to Paul by Epaphroditus to care for his needs while he was in prison (v. 18). He has already used the money as an object lesson on Christian contentment (vv. 11–13), but now, he wants to thank them and encourage them in a way that will also advance their sanctification in Christian giving. First, he speaks of them sharing in his distress. The Greek word translated "share" means an intensive fellowship with Paul in his suffering. Therefore, Christian giving draws us together in the sufferings of others, binding us together in the pain of life. Second, Paul uses the same Greek root to speak of their partnership (sharing together) in the work of the gospel. He notes that they had done this at the very beginning of his relationship with him, and now they were resuming their aid. Christian giving is a way of joining in the work of the gospel done by others. William Carey, before embarking on his trailblazing mission to India, said to his mission agency, "I will descend into the dark hole of heathenism, but you must hold the ropes for me."[2] "Holding the ropes" means partnering with Christian workers in their ministry, joining with them financially so they can do the work of advancing the gospel that we cannot do directly. Third, Christian giving is a matter of "giving and receiving" (v. 15). There is a marvelous give and take in the Christian life. Paul had poured out spiritual blessings on the Philippians—rich gospel instruction and prayer for them. Now, in a similar message to what he wrote

2. Quoted in Timothy George, *Faithful Witness: The Life and Mission of William Carey* (Birmingham: New Hope, 1991), 74.

to the Roman Christians, they owed it to him to partner with him financially (Rom 15:27). This is the same logic Paul uses for financially supporting pastors who do the work of the ministry. The congregation receives spiritual blessings, and they give material blessings in return. This "give and take" binds the body of Christ together. Fourth, we note the consistency of healthy Christian giving. This was a regular habit on the part of the Philippians, for he said they did it "once and again" (v. 16). God does not want us to give sporadically but as a matter of lifestyle, a consistent habit. Fifth, Christian giving stores up heavenly reward. Paul says he is ultimately looking not for the temporary gift of money but the crediting of their generosity in God's eternal record book. Jesus openly spoke of this storing up of treasure in heaven in Matthew 6:19–21 in the context of his teaching on money. He also said that when we give to the needy who cannot repay us in this world, we will be "repaid at the resurrection of the just" (Luke 14:14). For all eternity, we will be enjoying the compounded heavenly interest of all the giving we do here on earth. As Randy Alcorn said, "You can't take it with you, but you can send it on ahead."[3] The more generously we give now, the more treasure we will have in heaven. Sixth, Christian giving brings joy to others. See how happy Paul is in this part of the epistle. He is happy at every level—happy that his needs are met, happy that they love him enough to care about him, happy that they love Christ and the gospel so much, happy that they are storing up treasure in heaven. Seventh and more importantly, faith-filled Christian giving brings joy to God. God sees it as worship. Paul uses sacrificial language from the Old Testament, saying their gift is "a fragrant offering, a sacrifice acceptable and pleasing to God." How marvelous is

3. Randy Alcorn, *The Treasure Principle* (Sisters, OR: Multnomah, 2001), 17.

that: to please God so much by giving something as insignificant as money. Eighth, Christian giving is an exercise in faith, for it causes us to trust in a God who will meet our own needs if we give sacrificially to others, and the proportion God uses is infinite—"according to his riches in glory in Christ Jesus" (v. 19). The more we give by faith, the more we will see God do amazing things to meet our own needs. Ninth, Christian giving is done for the eternal glory of God, as are all things in the Christian life (v. 20).

REFLECT ON CHRIST

As I look over this list of elements of Christian giving, I realize how vital Christ is in every one of these elements. Ultimately, we give because Christ has first given everything for us. As Paul makes plain in 2 Corinthians 8:9, "For you know the grace of our Lord Jesus Christ, that though he was rich, yet for your sake he became poor, so that you by his poverty might become rich." It was Christ who taught us to give, and it is Christ whose Spirit enables us to give, and it is for the kingdom of Christ and his glory that all true giving is done.

APPLY GOD'S WORD

The application of today's text is clear. In the words of Jesus, "Give, and it will be given to you. Good measure, pressed down, shaken together, running over, will be put into your lap. For with the measure you use it will be measured back to you" (Luke 6:38). Go over each of the nine points listed above in prayer, then ask God what he wants you to do. He will most certainly lead you by his Spirit. Do not delay or make excuses. Give today, give by faith, and begin a journey of habitual Christian giving that will last the rest of your life on earth.

PRAY

Father, it is only by your amazing grace that we have anything at all, for all things belong to you and will go back to you in the end. Free us from the deceptive idolatry of money and help us to give as this passage teaches us. Amen.

STUDY IT FURTHER

1. Read the account of the giving that Israel did under David for the building of the temple that Solomon would make (1 Chr 29:1–9). Then read how David prays about their generosity (vv. 10–17). What do you learn from those verses about giving to the Lord?

2. What does Matthew 6:19–21 teach you about using money to store up treasure in heaven?

3. Research a Christian missions or aid ministry that you have never given to before and give as the Lord leads you.

Day 40

Philippians 4:21–23

READ

Greet every saint in Christ Jesus. The brothers who are with me greet you. All the saints greet you, especially those of Caesar's household. The grace of the Lord Jesus Christ be with your spirit.

MEDITATE

The book of Revelation gives us a stunning foretaste of the vast assembly of saints (Christians) who will gather around the throne of Christ in heaven:

> After this I looked, and behold, a great multitude that no one could number, from every nation, from all tribes and peoples and languages, standing before the throne and before the Lamb, clothed in white robes, with palm branches in their hands, and crying out with a loud voice, "Salvation belongs to our God who sits on the throne, and to the Lamb!" (Rev 7:9–10)

This innumerable multitude will have been won to Christ by the Holy Spirit, by the power of the gospel, and by the sacrificial witness of brothers and sisters. The stories that will be revealed in heaven of how they were rescued on earth will be astonishing. In that vision, the apostle John wrote the question, "These in white robes—who are they, and where did they come from?" (Rev 7:13 NIV). How amazing it will be to find out in perfect detail from the memory of God every answer to that question.

What will it be like for us to meet these brothers and sisters in heaven? What will it be like to hear their stories, how God's Spirit worked to transform their minds from paganism to pure gospel truth? We will learn how God used them in their generation to spread the gospel even more, leading relatives, neighbors, trading partners, soldiers, and even mocking Colosseum audience members to repentance and faith in Christ. Through each of these saints, a piece of God's story is written for his glory.

In our text today, Paul refers to the brethren "of Caesar's household." Back in chapter 1, Paul spoke of his arrest in Rome as giving him access to the praetorian guard (1:13). These were the most elite soldiers in the Roman army, hand-selected to be Caesar's personal bodyguards. It is quite likely that Philippians 4:22 implies that Paul won some of these men to Christ. Beyond that, it is possible that other close members of Caesar's family might have been won to faith in Christ. This was the beginning of the long, bloody, and ultimately glorious spiritual battle between Christ and Caesar that would culminate in the emperor Constantine declaring himself to be a Christian in the fourth century. Through courageous unseen witness by obscure merchants and slaves, the gospel spread as yeast through a large batch of dough (Matt 13:33). Occasionally, Roman procurators and emperors hostile to Christ would make anti-Christian laws and viciously persecute followers of Christ, but this only hastened the spread of the gospel. Jesus said, "Unless a grain of wheat falls into the ground and dies, it remains alone; but if it dies, it bears much fruit" (John 12:24). Tertullian captured this truth in his famous statement, "The blood of martyrs is seed."

REFLECT ON CHRIST

Paul's final word in this book is very familiar, for it is how he ends all his epistles: "The grace of our Lord Jesus Christ be with you all." Jesus Christ is a fountain of grace for all his people. As he said to the Samaritan woman at the well, "Whoever drinks of the water that I will give him will never be thirsty again. The water that I will give him will become in him a spring of water welling up to eternal life" (John 4:14). We are totally dependent on this limitless supply of grace flowing from Jesus—grace to cover all our sins, grace to continue transforming our hearts, grace to serve him fruitfully in our lives. The words of this magnificent epistle are an endless source of grace for us, as they have been for every generation of Christians over the last twenty centuries. As we come to the end of our forty-day journey through Philippians, resolve that it will not be the last time you drink of Christ's living water that flows from this particular fountain. Learn its lessons again and again, and they will focus your mind on the perfection of Christ and the eternal joy that is ours in him.

APPLY GOD'S WORD

As I look over this final paragraph in Philippians, I take away the practical command to greet the brothers and sisters I know with the richest of Christian greetings. It is more than just, "Say hello for me!" It involves using the powerful truths woven into the words of this epistle to enrich the souls of all the saints we know. It is especially poignant for those who are not immediately in our presence. Paul is reaching out to the saints in Philippi by means of this letter. We have far more means to connect with people in our digital age, even to the most distant parts of the globe, than Paul did. Do you know any missionaries serving in foreign lands? Resolve to greet them in the Lord today. There are so many ways by which you can bless their day. Let them know you love them in the Lord, that you are praying for them, that their walk with Christ is an inspiration to you. This is not just for missionaries but can be used for any Christian living far from you. Greet them in the name of the Lord and be a source of Christ's grace to them today.

PRAY

My gracious heavenly Father, this journey through
Philippians has been rich, a feast for my soul.
May its timeless lessons shape me as never before.
May I learn to live openly for Christ, yearning to
know him in all things, even in suffering. Amen.

STUDY IT FURTHER

1. What aspect of this journey through Philippians have you found most encouraging? What have you found most convicting? How has it helped your prayer life? How has it challenged you in witnessing? How has it helped you to grow in a passionate love for Christ?

2. If you could grow in one way mentioned in our study in Philippians, what would it be?

3. Share your thoughts about this great little epistle with someone at your church. Ask that person if he/she would like to study Philippians with you.

Group Reading Plan

What follows is a suggested plan for reading through this study in a group, with six days of study per week.

WEEK 1

1. Introduction to Philippians
2. Philippians 1:1–2
3. Philippians 1:3–5
4. Philippians 1:6
5. Philippians 1:7–8
6. Philippians 1:9–11

WEEK 2

1. Philippians 1:12
2. Philippians 1:13–14
3. Philippians 1:15–20
4. Philippians 1:21
5. Philippians 1:22–26
6. Philippians 1:27–30

WEEK 3

1. Philippians 2:1–4
2. Philippians 2:5–8
3. Philippians 2:9–11
4. Philippians 2:12
5. Philippians 2:13
6. Philippians 2:14–18

WEEK 4

1. Philippians 2:19–24
2. Philippians 2:25–28
3. Philippians 2:29–30
4. Philippians 3:1–3
5. Philippians 3:4–7
6. Philippians 3:8–9

WEEK 5

1. Philippians 3:10
2. Philippians 3:11
3. Philippians 3:12–14
4. Philippians 3:15–17
5. Philippians 3:18–19
6. Philippians 3:20

WEEK 6

1. Philippians 3:21
2. Philippians 4:1
3. Philippians 4:2–3
4. Philippians 4:4
5. Philippians 4:5
6. Philippians 4:6–7

WEEK 7

1. Philippians 4:8–9
2. Philippians 4:10–12
3. Philippians 4:13
4. Philippians 4:14–20
5. Philippians 4:21–23